Dirk Louis
Peter Müller

IN NO TIME

Java2

Prentice
Hall

An imprint of Pearson Education

PEARSON EDUCATION LIMITED

Head Office:
Edinburgh Gate
Harlow CM20 2JE
Tel: +44 (0)1279 623623
Fax: +44 (0)1279 431059

London Office:
128 Long Acre
London WC2E 9AN
Tel: +44 (0)20 7447 2000
Fax: +44 (0)20 7240 5771
Website: www.it-minds.com

First published in Germany in 2001
© Pearson Education Limited 2002

First published in 2001 as *Easy Java 2*
by Markt & Technik Buch und Software Verlag GmbH
Martin-Kollar-Straße 10-12
D-81829 Munich
Germany

This edition published 2002 by Pearson Education

British Library Cataloguing in Publication Data
A CIP catalogue record for this book can be obtained from the British Library.

ISBN 0-130-94941-8

10   9   8   7   6   5   4   3   2   1

Translated and typeset by Cybertechnics, Sheffield.
Printed and bound in Great Britain by Ashford Colour Press, Gosport, Hampshire.

The Publishers' policy is to use paper manufactured from sustainable forests.

600011052X

 **University of Hertfordshire**

College Lane, Hatfield, Herts. AL10 9AB

Learning and Information Services
College Lane Campus Learning Resources Centre, Hatfield

For renewal of Standard and One Week Loans,
please visit the web site **http://www.voyager.herts.ac.uk**

This item must be returned or the loan renewed by the due date.
The University reserves the right to recall items from loan at any time.
A fine will be charged for the late return of items.

Contents

✷ Chapter 9: Multiple execution of statements 121

✦ Chapter 10: Methods: bundling activities together 141

Chapter 11: Arrays – processing 1000 data elements at the same time 159

Preface

Are you interested in making computer programs on your own? Would you like to discover how a computer becomes something that is almost alive, able to show coloured pictures, make sounds and solve complex tasks for you?

Then you are holding the right book in your hands. This book explains simply and clearly how simple computer programs are created. You will learn how to program.

Programming is always based on what we call a programming language, which, just like any natural language, has many different variants. You may have heard about some of them before such, C++, Oberon, Python, Delphi or Java. Java is a modern programming language that you can learn relatively easily, without losing its functionality and efficiency. For this reason, Java has become a standard programming language that is progressively going to replace other established languages.

This book will try to make your approach to Java as easy as possible, without renouncing quality and well-grounded knowledge. Along with the actual components of the Java programming language, you will learn a lot about general techniques and modern software development. And you do not need any previous knowledge! It doesn't matter if you have never programmed before, because no software engineering background is required. You only need general computer knowledge in order to begin this course, i.e. you should already be familiar with Windows 98 or similar, and you should know, for instance, what the ⏎ (return) button is and what it does. Apart from this basic knowledge, you do not need to know anything about programming. This also means that we are not going to bombard you with technical terminology and jargon. Sometimes you cannot avoid technical terms, but they will always be explained and never introduced on the sly.

The authors wish you great fun and success in learning how Java programs work.

Dirk Louis, dirklouis@cs.com

Peter Müller, jp_mueller@web.de

Chapter 1

A brief introduction

*We begin with a brief introduction that will show you
the main aspects of the programming path with Java.*

In principle, Java programming consists of the use of four tools: the editor, the compiler, the interpreter and sometimes the debugger:

1. The Java program itself is written by means of a simple word-processing code – a so-called editor. The created program text (the program code) has to be rebuilt according to the rules (the syntax) of the respective programming language, in our case in accordance with the Java rules. We also call this program code "source code".

2. The source code is readable but has no value for a computer. It needs machine code (a sequence of zeros and ones) since its processor can only understand this (computers are actually stupid). In order to insert machine codes in the computer, you need a special program called a compiler that converts the source code into a machine code. However, compared with the other programming languages, Java shows a peculiarity here. The Java compiler does not convert the source code into a machine code, but into an intermediate form that is readable by both the human eye and the computer (the same is valid for the processor).

3. We submit this byte code to a special program, the interpreter. The interpreter reads the byte code and converts it bit by bit into machine code and lets the processor execute it.

4. It is quite difficult to create a program, and a finished program does not always do what the programmer actually wants it to. For the fault diagnosis, we use a special program called a debugger. Fault diagnosis and the removal of faults together are called "debugging".

So far, you have already learnt the fundamental steps of the programming path: we write the program as source code, compile it in the intermediate program called byte code, and execute it using an interpreter. Up to now everything is clear, but what does this source code contain?

To get a general idea, we will briefly mention the essential aspects of a program:

- Data input and output: a program needs data in all cases. Such data comes from the user (who types on the keyboard or clicks with the mouse) or from different sources, e.g. from a file on the hard disk. Therefore, the source code has to determine which data are to be handled, where data go, and how data are distributed (e.g. onto the screen, into a file or on the printer).

- Data processing: any data contained in the program have to be processed. Data can be calculated, searched, compared or modified. In addition to these operations, the programmer must pay attention as to how the data are organized and filed in the main memory of the computer during this processing.

- Program flow: in principle, the statements of a program are usually executed by the computer step by step and one after the other, from start to finish. However, we can also control this sequential program flow; basically, it is carried out on loops – statement blocks that are worked on – and branchings, in which just one of many alternatives is developed.

You will find the details about these issues in the following chapter. Since Java is a very extensive language, we will focus only on the most important elements that are necessary to create the first simple programs. Let's begin!

Chapter 2

What are programs?

So far, you probably only know programs from a user's perspective. You can write letters and other documents by means of a word-processing program, organise addresses or a CD collection with a database program, and surf the Internet thanks to a browser. But where do these programs come from? What is the difference between a program and a text document? How can you write your own programs? This chapter will answer all these questions.

What is a program?

There are people who almost stand to attention with reverence when faced with a computer. If these people ask the computer to give them the name of the capital of Nepal and get Lhasa as an answer, they will accept this answer without hestitation, because they think that computers are infallible. Yet, Lhasa is the capital of Tibet, not Nepal.

So are computers stupid? No, because the mistake in the example above is not made by the computer itself, but by a program that is executed by the computer. Computers are neither intelligent nor stupid. They are nothing but devices that play programs. So, in the same way as you insert music CDs in your CD player and then play them, you install programs on a computer which you then execute.

There is a slight difference, however.

On a music CD, there are data (tones and harmonies) that the CD player plays in succession. A program, on the other hand, contains commands that are to be executed by the computer.

Figure 2.1: You must feed data and programs into the computer.

Do you speak computerese?

Wow! Programs contain commands. We should first consider the meaning of this sentence. Can we execute a command such as "Name the capital of Nepal" on a program on the computer and get the answer "Kathmandu" back? No, because if it were so easy, programmers would not be so well paid.

The problem is that the computer only understands a specific sequence of elementary commands, such as:

"Copy the contents of the memory cell 325 to memory cell 326"

"Copy the contents of the memory cell 12 to register A"

"Add the value 1 to the content to register A"

To make things worse, these commands need to be coded as a sequence of zeros and ones. These binary coded commands are called *machine codes*. Can you imagine having to draft your programs as machine code?

```
0011001100111010
0011000100100101
1111011001101100
```

Brrrr!

Well, what must you do? You get a conversion program, also called a *compiler*, which converts commands into machine code. The compiler itself is not capable of converting commands such as "Name the capital of Nepal" into machine code, though. The compiler requires the commands to be drafted in a special language, a programming language. And as you may have already expected, the programming language we will adopt in this text to create programs is Java.

Byte code

Compared with other languages such as C++, Java shows an unusual feature: the Java compiler converts a series of Java commands (the Java program) not into the machine code as above, but into an intermediate form called *byte code*. However, this intermediate stage is not much easier to read.

9

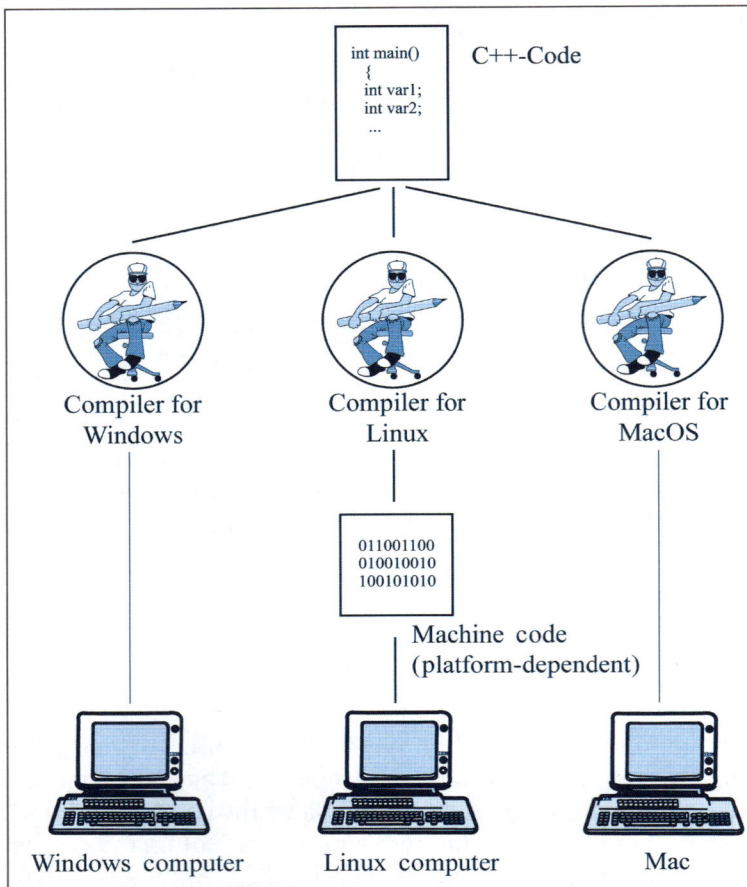

Figure 2.2: A compiled C++ program can only be executed on the computer platform it was created for.

At this point, the issue is platform independence. A program can be used independently of the operating system. You probably know that there are many different operating systems, such as Windows 98 or Linux or MacOS on Apple computers. These operating systems are not compatible with each other, and therefore you cannot, for instance, execute a game (let's call it risk.exe) for Windows 98 on a Linux system. The risk.exe file consists of a machine code that is coordinated with the respective operating system (Windows 98 in our example) and the processor type used (Intel Pentium). If the game were programmed in Java, this problem would not arise. It would appear in the intermediate form we have already mentioned, called byte code, and would run on any operating system, provided that there is a small relief program that lists the bytecode file, converts it line by line into a machine code and submits it to the processor to be executed. We call this process interpretation and, as a result, the relief program is called the interpreter.

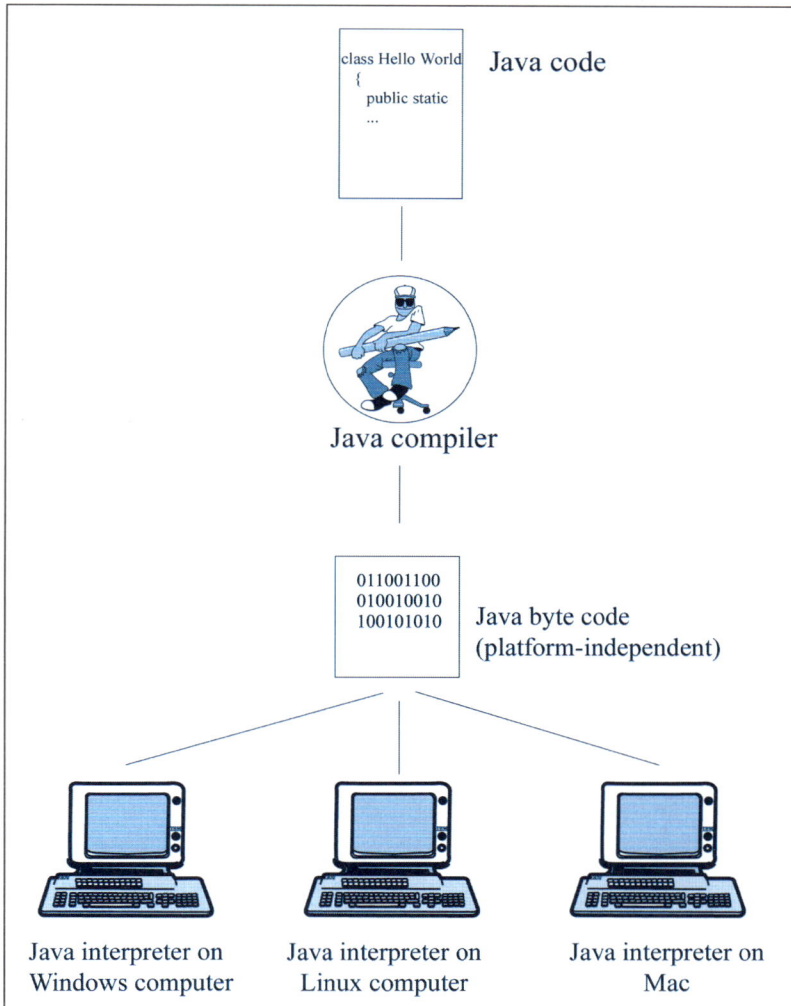

Figure 2.3: A compiled Java program can be executed by means of a suitable interpreter on any platform.

From concept to program

Let's take another look at how we can arrive at a program that can tell us the capital of Nepal, or any other country. How can such a program be created?

To begin with, the program should know the capital of each country. For this, you could list all countries with their capitals in the program code. Even if this was possible in principle, since a program can also contain data in addition to the commands, it is better, when dealing with a large quantity of data, to insert data into a separate file. This file, which could even be a simple text file, serves as a database to the program.

At the start of the program, the program should ask the user to indicate the country whose capital he/she wants to know. The program reads the user's input, opens the database, and checks all the contents of the database until it finds the corresponding country. Then it checks which capital belongs to this country. After this, the program closes the database and shows the user the matching capital it has found.

This kind of process for the work of a program is defined as an algorithm. Put a bit more clearly, the algorithm looks like this:

1. Ask the user to enter a country.

2. Read the user's input.

3. Open the database.

4. Check the inputs in the database of the series and compare each country saved there with the one you are searching. When doing so, two things are possible:

   - A corresponding input is sometimes found. Break off your search, read the corresponding capital and output it on the screen.[1]

   - You reach the end of the database without achieving the latter point. A corresponding error message is output on the screen.

---

1. A note on the infallibility of the computer again: it should be clear that this program does not return the actual capital of the country, but rather what is stored in the database as "the capital" of the country searched. If we search the capital of Nepal, and Kathmandu is recorded as the capital of Nepal, the program provides a correct answer. If the programmer who set up the database made a typing error, Kathmandu or Lhasa may well be associated with Nepal in the database. If this is the case, then the program will return Kathmandu or Lhasa as the capital of Nepal – until someone notices the error and corrects the entry in the database.

5. Close the database.

> **NOTE**
>
> *Now you may be thinking, "Goodness, I would never have been able to understand this on my own," and wondering how you will ever learn to formulate algorithms. You can learn it quite simply with the programming language. A well-formulated algorithm not only indicates how a program runs, but also knows how the program is implemented, i.e. it uses the same typical elements and constructions that are also used in the program code. You will learn more about these elements and constructions (loops, branchings, file operations) in the course of this book.*
>
> *Moreover, dealing with small programs, you can avoid algorithms, assuming that you already have a little experience of programming. With larger programs on the other hand, we suggest not to simply program away, but first to create a process plan for your program.*

The next step is to convert the algorithm into program code. Therefore, from the example above, we should get to know how to set up a Java program, read Java files in the hard disk of the computer, program a loop (to search data in the database), code branchings and much more.

Since you will learn all these things in the course of the book, we will skip this stage without further ado and simply assume that we have already input the complete Java source text of the program into a text editor and saved it on the hard disk as a file called `Countries.java`.

Now, let's call the compiler and submit to it the file with our Java code. The compiler will now check whether the Java code is syntactically correct, i.e. if it is structured according to the rules of the Java language. If nothing is wrong, it converts the Java code into a byte code and saves it in a new file (whose content can no longer be read by means of a normal editor). This file shows a specific ending, namely `.class`. In order to execute the program, as already mentioned, this `Countries.class` file needs to be submit to a Java interpreter.

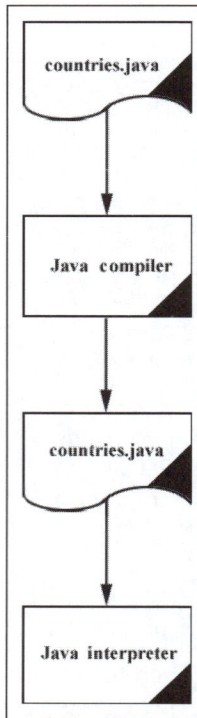

Figure 2.4: Development of the program creation.

Windows®, windows and consoles

Many users, particularly younger people who have grown up with Windows 95/98 or NT, expect a program to provide a window with menu bars, tool bars, viewports, scroll bars, status bars and other interface elements. In other words, when they think of programs, they think of Windows Explorer, Netscape Navigator, WinZip, RealPlayer, Paint or whatever else they use.

But programs do not automatically work with windows (lucky for us beginners, because window utilities and support are really complex, and they are not necessary to learn a programming language to begin with.)

So why do so many programs have windows?

The answer is that windows make programs more user friendly. Almost all programs are dependent on the fact that they exchange information with the user. So the capital city program that we discussed in the previous chapter takes the name of a country from the user and returns the appropriate capital city as an answer.

A program that is to run under Windows (or X Window on UNIX/Linux systems) would produce a window for the interaction with the user, for example with a text field in which the user can type the name of the country, a button that the user clicks with a mouse in order to allow the program to search for the capital city, and another text field in which the capital city that is found is displayed.

WHAT IS THIS?

Since windows, dialogue boxes and interface elements such as menus, status bars, control elements etc. are used to interact with the user (amongst other things), they are described together as the graphical user interface *(GUI).*

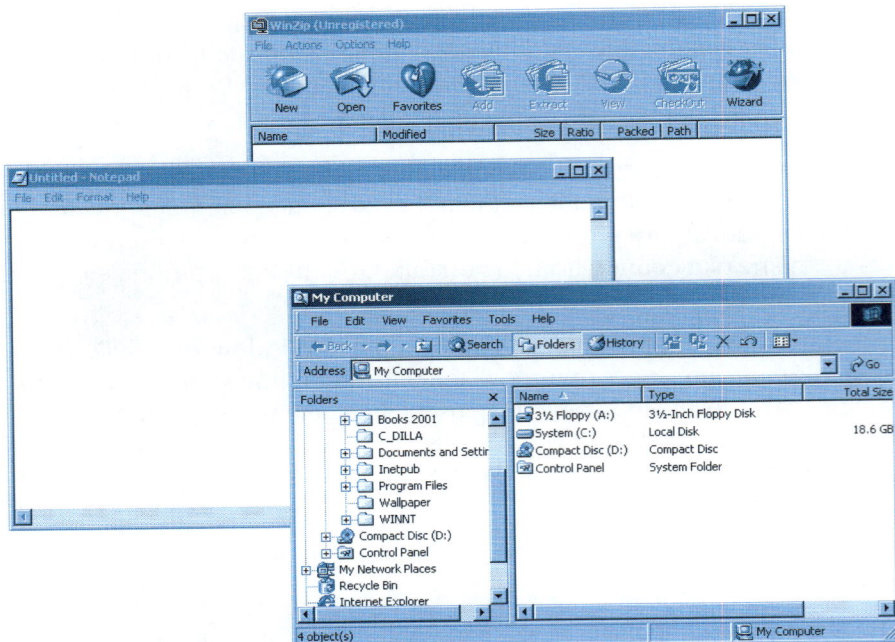

Figure 2.5: GUI programs in Windows.

A program that does not run under Windows uses a *console* for the input and output of data.

Once, the computer itself was the console. Users sat in front of a black screen (even earlier still with green or brown text) and were presented with a *prompt*. They could type in commands using the keyboard which were executed by the computer after sending with the ⏎ (return) key. In addition to common operating system commands, such as the change of current directories or the deletion of a file, programs can also be called up from the console. The console then takes this on and uses these to issue results or query the data given by the user.

Since then, things have changed and people are used to finding a graphic Window interface on PCs. The console has not disappeared, however. It can be called up by the Window interface where it appears in its own window. In Linux, the console is called console or terminal, according to the Window Manager that is being used. In Windows 95/98 it is normally called MS-DOS prompt and can be called up by the START/PROGRAM menu.

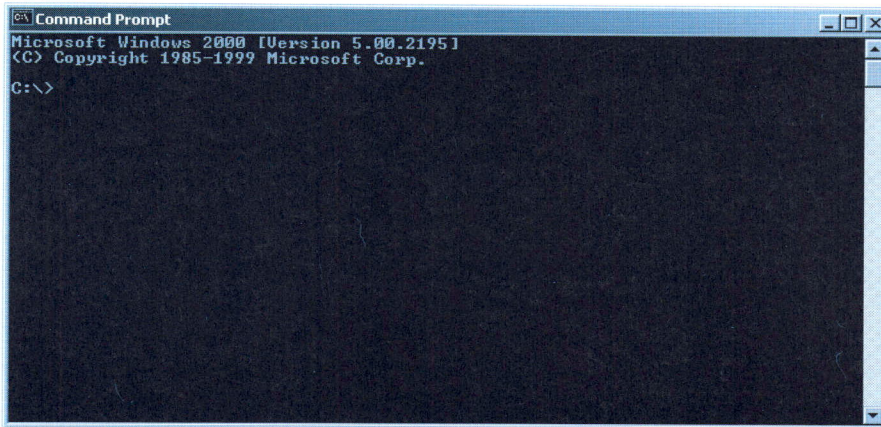

Figure 2.6: The MS-DOS prompt (console in Windows).

For us, as beginners in programming, it is an advantage if we can just focus on the console programs. Anyone wanting to write actual window-based programs needs to work hard on the creation of the GUI. Java offers extensive support of windows, buttons and the mouse, but it can be really tricky to create a graphic interface. Therefore, as a beginner, your aim is to learn the core language.

All Java?

If you have already had a look at some computer magazines, you will almost certainly have noticed that many concepts are related to Java, for example the JDK 1.3 or J2SDK Standard Edition. But if you also consider further articles discussing JavaScript, JavaBeans and Enterprise JavaBeans (often abbreviated to J2EE) you could become somewhat confused.

But now you have this book, let's clear things up.

The first clear distinction we can make is between the programming language *Java* and the script language *JavaScript*. The latter is not a proper programming language, but, as the name indicates, it is a script language for small programs (the so-called *scripts*) that are sometimes used in HTML pages.[2]

---

2. HTML is a format in which all Web pages are defined.

On the other hand, (Enterprise) JavaBeans is "proper" Java and, in addition to "normal" Java, it also provides certain mechanisms and tools for professional software development in the commercial field.

"Normal" Java is the subject of this book. Since Java has been around for many years and has been constantly developing ever since its inception, there are different versions of the Java standard, which is usually defined as *JDK* (Java Development Kit). This began in 1993 with the JDK 1.0, then came the 1.02, the 1.1 and so on, until the 1.1.8. Later, the company Sun (the inventor of Java) thought that this numbering could become boring in the long term and did not name the following version JDK 1.2 but J2SDK SE[3] Version 1.2. The up-to-date version (March 2001) is, by the way, the J2SDK standard edition version 1.3 and will be dealt with in this book. But back to the name. In practice, we normally use JDK 1.3, so we prefer to do the same in this book.

Programming is fun

Before you go onto the next chapter, we would like to congratulate you again on your decision to learn to program with Java. Programming is a fascinating activity. It challenges our logical skills as well as our creativity. It is fun, it can make you money, and it gives you the satisfaction of having created your own work.

Of course, it can also be frustrating at times. But if it was not difficult sometimes, then the pleasure of arriving at your goal would not be so great. Just imagine the frustration and pleasure of the keen programmer who, during his or her programming career, has spent many a night lying awake trying to identify the error that causes the program to crash, and finally finds it? If you learn to love programming, then you may well release skills you have never dreamed of.

---

3. SE = Standard Edition.

Anyone wanting to learn how to program must also be aware that things do not always go smoothly. This is not anybody's fault, and you must not blame yourself. This book should introduce you to Java programming in a way that is fun and, whenever possible, frustration-free. However, if any difficulty arises, e.g. if you have not understood something completely or you end up with a program that does not run, stop for a while, carry on reading the text or take a day off. Problems often become clear by themselves. If you cannot get further and are about to despair, then email us (dirklouis@cs.com, jp_mueller@web.de).

Chapter 3

Creating your own programs

In this chapter, you will learn more about tools. We begin with the installation of the Java development systems (JDK) and the equipment of your computer for program development through the JDK. Finally, we will create and analyse our first program, and see how the program files are organised on the hard disk.

Installing the JDK

Everything that we have seen in the program creation with Java – except for the editor for the drafting of the program source texts – can be found in the Java Development Kit (JDK). You can download the JDK free of charge from the Java Web site `http://java.sun.com` (found under the name `J2SDK Standard Edition`). You can find the up-to-date version of this text on the accompanying CD in the directory *JDK*.

File	Description
`CDROM:\JDK\ j2sdk1_3_0win.exe`	Setup file for Windows
`CDROM:\JDK\ j2sdk-1_3_0_02linux.bin`	Setup file for Linux
`CDROM:\JDK\ j2sdk1_3_0doc.zip`	ZIP file with additional Java reference in HTML format

Table 3.1: Content of the JDK directories in the book CD.

Before installing the JDK, close all the running applications. Installation programs (also called setup programs) are very sensitive in Windows 98/ME and can interfere with other applications that are being executed at the same time.

The actual installation of Microsoft Windows is very simple.

> **NOTE**
>
> *For the installation of the JDK and the creation of your own programs in Linux, follow the same steps that we used in Windows – but usually using other files, commands, etc. In the step-by-step instructions, pay attention to the Linux-specific notes.*

1 Insert the book CD-ROM into your disk drive.

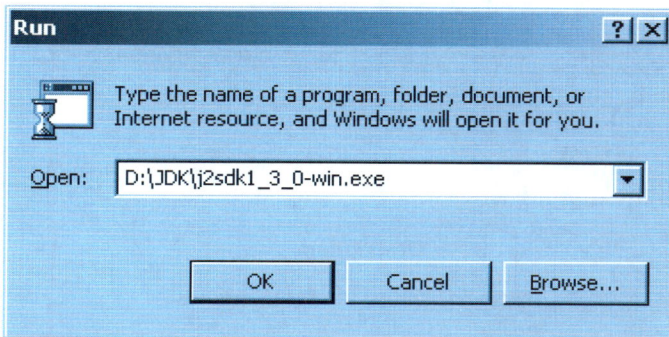

Figure 3.1: The setup program for Windows.

2 Execute the setup program.

Open the Windows START menu and choose the menu entry EXECUTE. The setup program for the Windows version itself is called `j2sdk1_3_0-win.exe` and is contained on the CD-ROM in the directory JDK. If your CD disk drive is set up, e.g. as disk drive `D:\` then enter `D:\JDK\j2sdk1_3_0-win.exe` into your dialogue window (Figure 3.1).

Or click on the BROWSE button and select the setup program that appears in the dialogue window.

Finally, by clicking on the OK button, you start the installation program.

> **NOTE**
>
> *The setup program for Linux is called* `j2sdk-1_3_0_02-linux.bin`.
> *Copy the file in the directory in which the JDK has to be installed (for example* `/home/yourname/java`). *To start the program, open a console (also called terminal window), and change to the directory in which the setup program is contained and type in:*
>
> `./j2sdk-1_3_0_02-linux.bin`

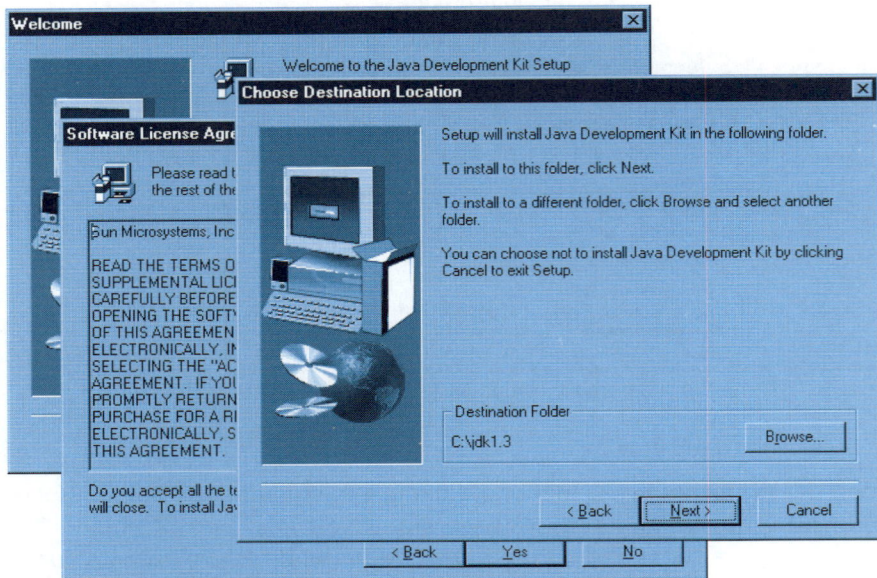

Figure 3.2: The welcome, software licence agreement and destination location windows.

3 Answer the questions that the installation program asks.

Now the welcome window of the installation assistant, the licence agreement and the query of the installation size and the target directory appear, one after the other (Figure 3.2). Accept the initial setting and click on the confirmation selection (depending on the window YES, ACCEPT, NEXT or FINISH).

At the end of the installation, your hard disk will lose about 30–60 MB of free memory, but you now have the J2SDK Standard Edition Version 1.3.

If you check your hard disk with Windows Explorer, you will find a new directory c:\jdk1.3 (i.e. the directory you have selected during the installation) that contains many subdirectories (Figure 3.3). Here, you can find all necessary files and programs that you will need to create programs using Java.

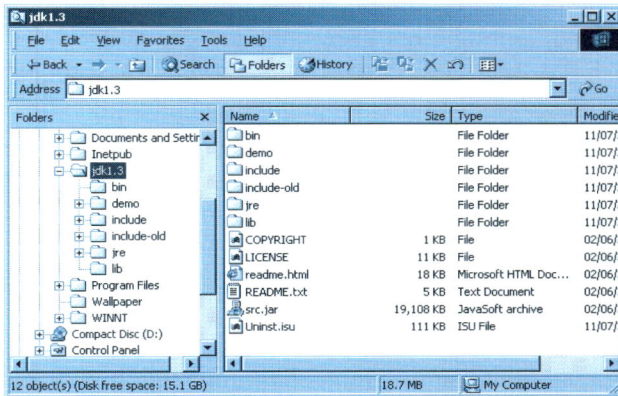

Figure 3.3: The JDK installed on the hard disk.

> **NOTE**
>
> *The Linux version is installed in the subdirectory* `jdk1.3.0_02`.

Further preparatory steps

The JDK is now installed. However, before we get cracking, we should check that all the tools necessary for programming are ready for use. We will consider:

- how to set up our system so that we are able to call the Java development tools from any directory;

- how to create a directory for our programs;

- how to choose a suitable editor.

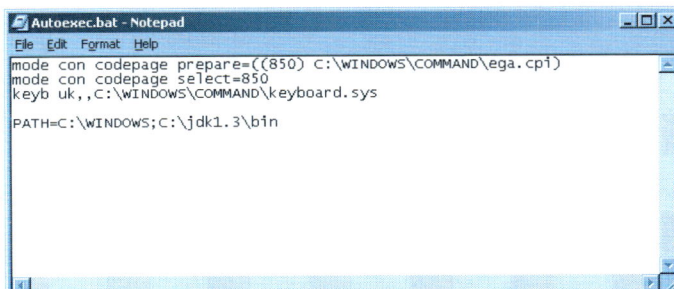

Figure 3.4: The JDK installed on the hard disk.

25

4 Type in the Java development tools into your system path (see Figure 3.4).

To create programs, we need, among other things, the Java compiler `javac` and the Java interpreter `java` that were copied into the JDK subdirectory `/bin` during the installation.

These programs are called by means of the console. In Windows, you open the console using the START menu entry PROGRAMS/ACCESSORIES/COMMAND PROMPT.[1] Using the program name and the path that leads to the program, you can call the Java development tools from the console. The program then outputs a short reference for its correct use (see Figure 3.5).[2]

WHAT IS THIS?

You can feed some operating system commands using the console and execute programs that – like the Java development tools – do not have a graphic user interface and do not work together with the window manager of the Windows system.

Using the console, you can also move within the directory structure of the computer (we will introduce the accompanying CD instructions in detail later). The directory in which you are working is usually shown on the left side of the prompt (it depends on the operating system which directory you are in after you have called the console).

It is annoying to type the path over and over again, so we want to set our system so that it can find the Java development tools automatically (then we simply need to type in `javac` or `java` in the console). Therefore, we have to include the JDK `bin` directory in the search path of the operating system. In the following explanations, we have assumed that you have installed the JDK in the directory `C:\jdk1.3`.

---

1. According to the Windows version, the console is also called in the START/ PROGRAMS /MS-DOS PROMPT or START/PROGRAMS/ACCESSORIES/COMMAND PROMPT.
2. Most operating systems enable the users to configure the prompt according to their preference.

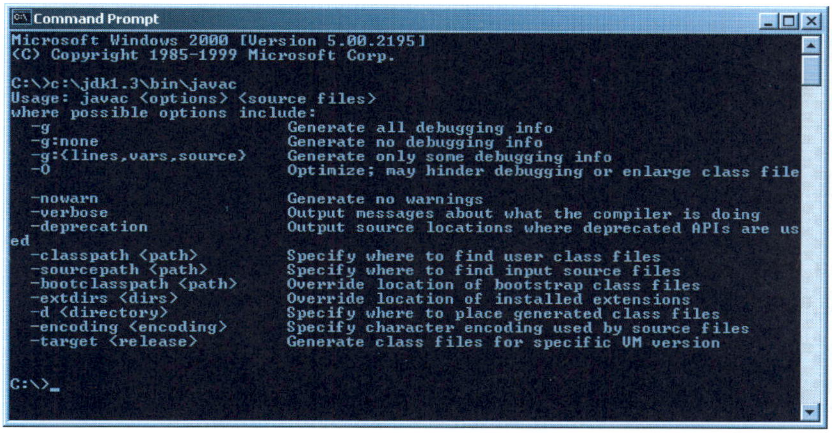

Figure 3.5: Calling the javac compiler from the Windows console.

Load the system file `c:\autoexec.bat` in a text editor (for example START/PROGRAMS/ACCESSORIES/EDITOR) and search for a PATH entry there. Add a semicolon and the JDK bin directory to this.

WHAT IS THIS?

The file autoexec.bat, which has to be contained in the directory `C:\`, is a batch file that is automatically executed with the start-up of the Windows operating system. You can write specific instructions and details for configuring the system in `autoexec.bat`.

For instance, if your `autoexec.bat` contains the following path entry:

`PATH=.;c:\;c:\dos;c:\windows`

you can extend it to:

`PATH=.;c:\;c:\dos;c:\windows;c:\jdk1.3\bin`

NOTE

If you cannot find any PATH instruction, insert a new PATH statement, such as `PATH=c:\jdk1.3\bin`. You may have to create the `autoexec.bat` file again.

After that, restart the computer and check whether you can call javac or java from any of the directories (see Figure 3.6).

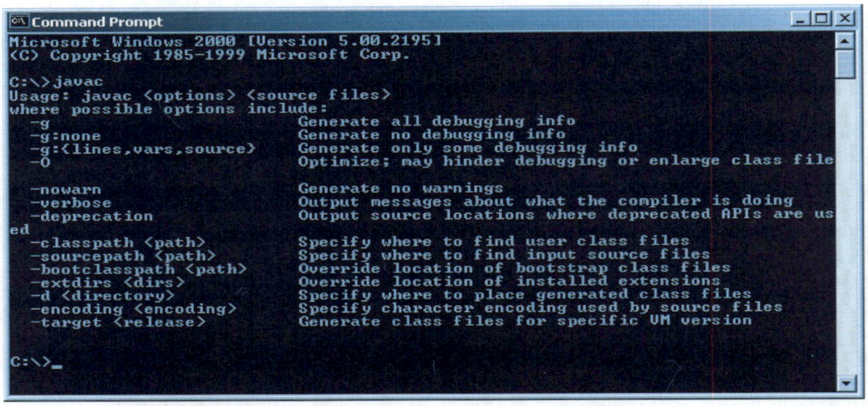

Figure 3.6: Calling the Java compiler without any path entry.

> **NOTE**
>
> *In Linux, manual adaptation of the system path should not be necessary. But, if needed, proceed in the same way. Search the path entry in the corresponding* `ini` *file (according to the configuration* `.login`, `.profile`, `.tcshrc` *etc.) and insert the* `Java bin` *directory, e.g.* `/home/yourname/jdk1.3/bin` *into the next line after the previous path entry:*
>
> ```
> set path = (/home/myname/jdk1.3/bin $path)
> ```

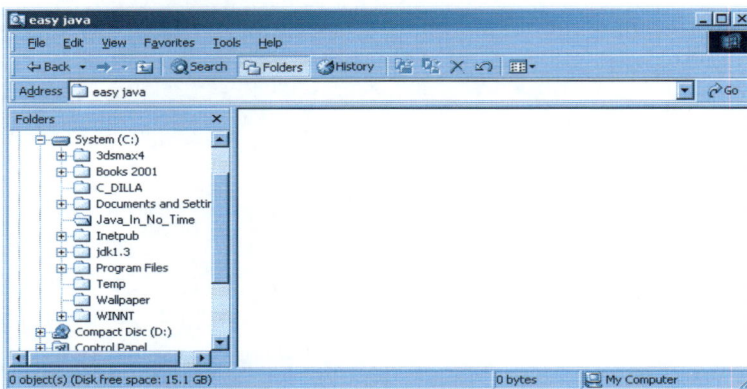

Figure 3.7: Creating the directory `Java_In_No_Time`.

5 Create a directory for the programs.

To create our own programs, we also need a suitable place where the corresponding Java files can be stored. In the rest of the book, we will assume that there is a directory `c:\Java_In_No_Time`. Therefore, using Windows Explorer (START/PROGRAMS/ACCESSORIES/WINDOWS EXPLORER) create such a directory (command FILE/NEW/FOLDER) (Figure 3.7).

> **NOTE**
>
> *In Linux, you can create the directory with a suitable file manager or open a console window and use the shell command* `mkdir directory name`.

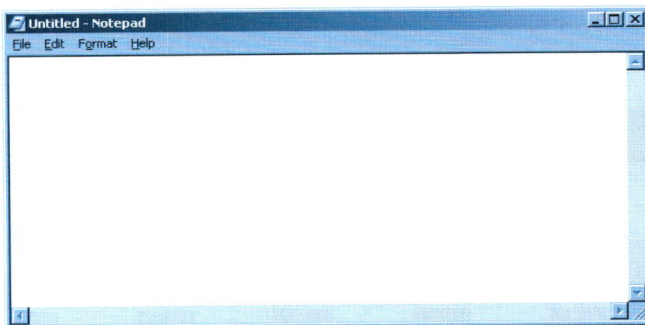

Figure 3.8: Opening Notepad.

6 Select an editor to set up the program source text.

To conclude, we need a word-processing program to create the Java source code files. For this purpose, there are special *editors,* but, for the purpose of this book, you just need the simple Windows editor *Notepad*, which you can call in START/PROGRAMS/ACCESSORIES/NOTEPAD (FIGURE 3.8). Of course, you can also use a full-blown word-processing program such as Word 2000 or StarOffice. It is important that when saving you select the function SAVE UNDER and select ONLY TEXT as the file type.

> **NOTE**
>
> *In Linux, you can use, for instance, vi or KEdit (if you are working with the KDE interface).*

29

We have now made all the essential preparations, and we can start creating the first program!

The first program

Now things become more complex. We begin to write up the Java source text.

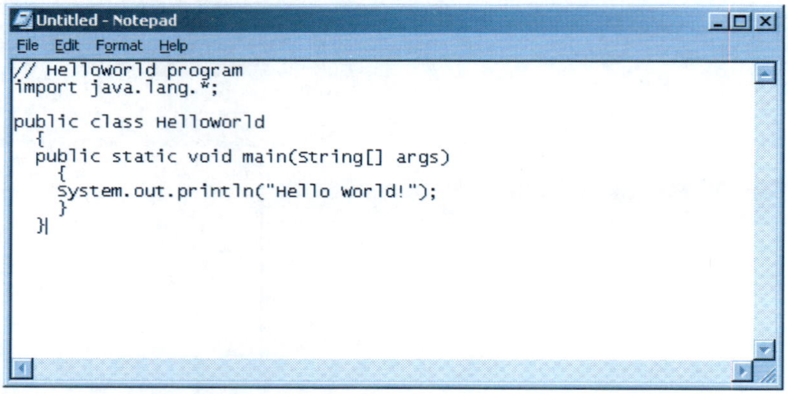

Figure 3.9: Beginning to write up the Java source.

1 Create a new file and type in the following program text.

```
// HelloWorld program
import java.lang.*;

public class HelloWorld
   {
   public static void main(String[] args)
      {
      System.out.println("Hello World!");
      }
   }
```

Input this source code exactly as is printed here. The semicolon at the end of the `println`-line is particularly important (Figure 3.9).

> **NOTE**
>
> *In Java, there is a difference between capitalization and lower-case printing. If, for instance, you type* `Main()` *in place of* `main()` *an error will occur.*

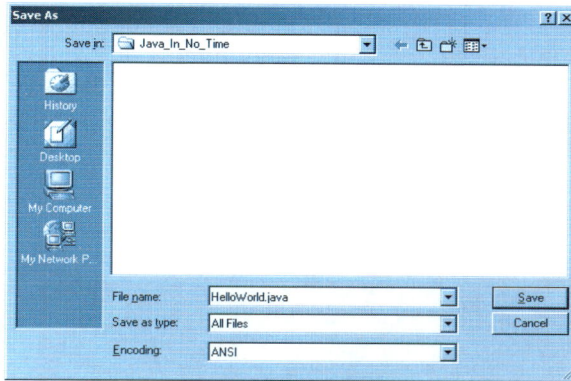

Figure 3.10: Saving the source code.

2 Save the source code.

At this point, you need to save the source code. Use `HelloWorld.java` (pay attention to the capitalization and lower case) as the file name, and `c:\Java_In_No_Time`, and the directory as suggested above.

> **NOTE**
>
> *Some word-processing programs add the ending* `.txt`. *If so, you need to change the file name in Windows Explorer manually, and clear the .txt again (select the file, then right click and select RENAME).*

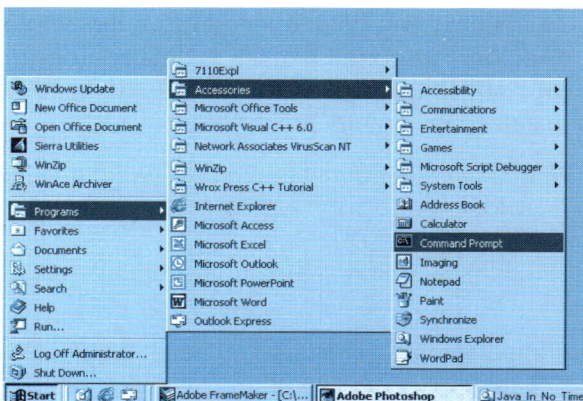

3 Open a console.

The next step in the development process is the compilation of the Java source text into the intermediate code (byte code). For this purpose, we need the Hi Java compiler; unfortunately this is not a graphic application and has no window. Therefore, we should first open the Windows console (the MS-DOS prompt). You can find it in the START bar (START/PROGRAMS/MS-DOS PROMPT).[3]

```
C:\>cd Java_In_No_Time
C:\Java_In_No_Time>_
```

Figure 3.11: Changing the directory.

If the console appears, you need to change to the work directory desired using the `cd` command (*change directory*). In our example, this would therefore be `c:\Java_In_No_Time`. Type `cd Java_In_No_Time` and press the ⏎ key.

If you wish to change to a subdirectory, you do not need to give the whole path, just the detail of the directory is enough (Figure 3.11). In order to change, for example, from the `c:\` directory to the directory `C:\Java_In_No_Time`, you just need the command:

`cd Java_In_No_Time`

If you want to change to a superordered directory, type in

`cd ..`

---

3. Depending on the Windows version, the console is also called via START/PROGRAMS/ PROMPT or START/PROGRAMS/ACCESSORIES/PROMPT.

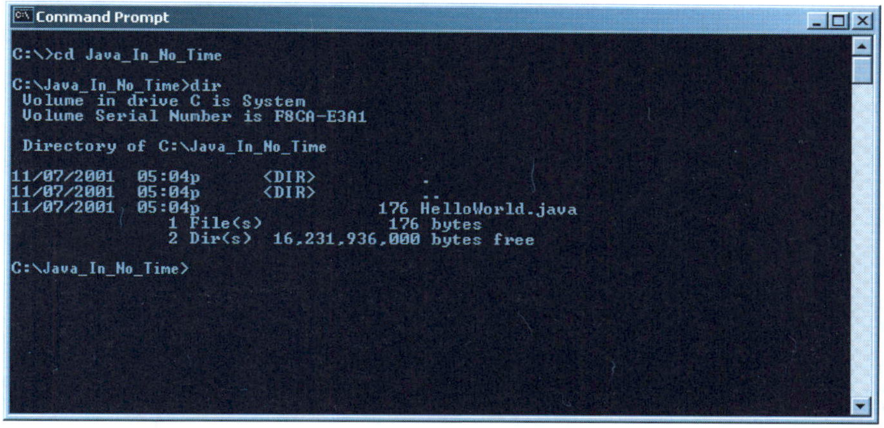

Figure 3.12: Listing the content of a directory.

Another important command that you can use is `dir` (*directory*). This shows the content of the up-to-date directory (Figure 3.12). If you want to list the files and subdirectories of the up-to-date directory page by page, use the command `dir /p`.

> **NOTE**
>
> *In Linux, the console commands used to change and list the directories are* `cd` *and* `ls`.

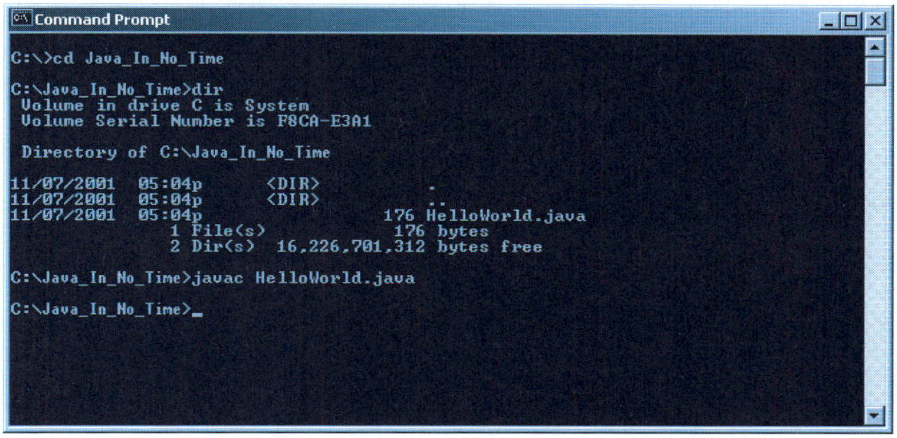

Figure 3.13: Compiling the source text.

4 Compile the source text.

The next step in the development process is the compilation of the Java source text. The Java compiler has the fairly straightforward name of *javac* and is called by the console. It expects the name of the Java file to be compiled as a parameter. In our example, the command is therefore `javac HelloWorld.java`.

If you now check the content of the directories with the `dir` command, you will see that a new file called `HelloWorld.class` has been created. It contains the byte code (Figure 3.13).

```
Command Prompt                                                     _ □ ×

C:\>cd Java_In_No_Time

C:\easy java>dir
 Volume in drive C is System
 Volume Serial Number is F8CA-E3A1

 Directory of C:\Java_In_No_Time

11/07/2001  05:04p       <DIR>           .
11/07/2001  05:04p       <DIR>           ..
11/07/2001  05:04p              176 HelloWorld.java
               1 File(s)           176 bytes
               2 Dir(s)  16,226,701,312 bytes free

C:\Java_In_No_Time>javac HelloWorld.java

C:\Java_In_No_Time>java HelloWorld
Hello World!

C:\Java_In_No_Time
```

Figure 3.14: Executing the program.

5 Execute the program.

The byte code can only be submitted to the Java interpreter to execute it. The Java interpreter is also a console program and is simply called `java`. As a parameter, it requires the name of the `.class` file that has to be executed, but without the ending `.class`. The execution of our first program is carried out as `java HelloWorld`.

After sending `java HelloWorld` and pressing the ⏎ key, the `Hello World!` entry will appear on the console after a few seconds. This is the sign that your first Java program is alive and kicking, and has been executed successfully (Figure 3.14).

Eliminating syntax mistakes

When drafting the source text, it is hard to avoid mistakes. It is often silly typing mistakes that make things difficult for Java beginners. The so-called "syntactical mistakes" are quite harmless, since they – as opposed to conceptual mistakes – are discovered by the compiler and are usually clearly identified.

Syntactical errors occur if the source text does not follow the rules of the programming language – in this case, Java. However, there are also conceptual mistakes that become noticeable when the program does compile without any errors, but, during execution, it fails to do what the programmer actually wanted.

While these conceptual mistakes are sometimes very difficult to identify, things definitely become easier with regards to syntactical mistakes, thanks to the Java compiler. As soon as it notices an error in the Java syntax, it issues a corresponding error message and interrupts the compilation. A lot of syntactical mistakes are typing errors, e.g. the misuse of a semicolon, which must appear after every statement.[4]

Syntactical errors, and therefore error messages, occur frequently during the compilation. We will simulate the error situation here. In order to simulate an error, modify the source text from the previous section, for example, by deleting the semicolon at the end of the `println()` statement. Save the new file again and start a compiling interconnection by calling `javac HelloWorld.java` in the MS-DOS prompt.

> **TIP**
>
> *Sometimes, a syntactical error produces many error messages. Always correct only the first mistake and, then compile the source text again. The subsequent mistakes sometimes disappear automatically.*

You will get the result shown in Figure 3.15:

---

4. You will find further details of this in the following chapters.

```
Command Prompt                                                    _|□|X|
C:\Java_In_No_Time>
C:\Java_In_No_Time>javac HelloWorld.java
HelloWorld.java:8: ';' expected
    System.out.println("Hello World!")
                                      ^
1 error

C:\Java_In_No_Time>_
```

Figure 3.15: The compiler encountered an error.

`javac` has recognised that the semicolon is missing after the last bracket of the `println()` statement. This is also shown with a ^ in its error message. Also helpful is the statement `HelloWorld.java:8`, which indicates that the error occured in line 8 of the source code file `HelloWorld.java`. On the basis of this information, remove the mistake and you can then compile with no further errors.[5]

Structuring files

During the course of this book you will create your own Java programs. In the long run, it will be unwieldy to save all `.java` and `.class` files in the same directory. Therefore, we suggest that you create a subdirectory for each individual program in the `Java_In_No_Time` directory.

For the example above, we will create the subdirectory `HelloWorld` and move there the files `HelloWorld.java` and `HelloWorld.class` that are already available. For these actions, you can use either Windows Explorer (you surely already know this) or commands to be given in the console. Because you have to work with the console in any case, we will briefly mention the necessary steps:

1 Change the directory with the cd command, where a subdirectory has to be created.

---

5. Another frequent mistake is making new errors when eliminating an old one!

Since we are already in the directory `Java_In_No_Time`, this step is no longer necessary.

2 Create the new directory using the command `md`.

This command expects the name of the directory that has to be created as a parameter; therefore, in this case, type in: `md HelloWorld`.

> **TIP**
>
> *If you want to execute a command that had already been typed in previously in the console, just press the ⬆ key until the command appears in the console. By means of the ⬅ and ➡ keys you can move into the instruction line and edit the mistake before sending it off, pressing the ⏎ key .*

3 Move the files `HelloWorld.java` and `HelloWorld.class` into the subdirectory using the command `move`.

The command `move` requires the name of the file that has to be moved as first parameter, and the name of the target directory as second parameter, i.e. `move HelloWorld.java HelloWorld` and `move HelloWorld.class HelloWorld` (Figure 3.16).[6]

> **NOTE**
>
> *If you wish to copy rather than move, use the command `copy` instead of `move`. The parameters stay the same: first the "source", then the "target".*

---

6. In Windows 95/98, you need to explicitly activate the recording of the given command line instructions. After starting the console, enter the command `doskey` at the prompt or write the command `doskey` directly in the `autoexec.bat`.

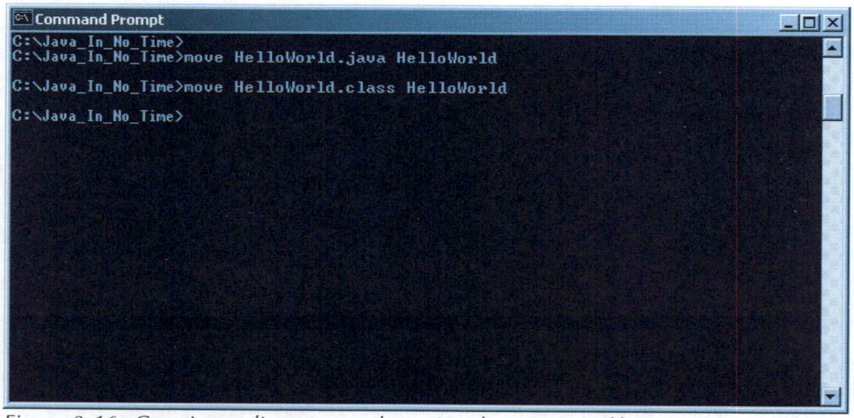

Figure 3.16: Creating a directory and moving the previous files.

If you now check the content of the up-to-date directory `Java_In_No_Time` with the `dir` command, you will notice that the files have disappeared and a new directory *HelloWorld* is available instead (Figure 3.17). Therefore, change to this subdirectory by means of `cd HelloWorld` and display the content using `dir`.

Figure 3.17: The new directory with the copied files.

> **NOTE**
>
> In Linux, the corresponding commands are `mv` (for move) and `cp` (for copy).

Chapter 4

The first program

There are a number of typical elements that are
common to almost all Java programs.
This chapter will look at these elements in detail.

The program code

Before looking at the program elements individually, we should take a look at the whole source text of a program:

```
// Hello World Program
import java.lang.*;

public class Hello World
  {
  public static void main(String[] args)
    {
    System.out.println("Hello World!");
    }
  }
```

Do you recognise this? This is the same program we used in Chapter 3 to test our compiler. In Chapter 3 we typed it in without analysing it; here we want to take a closer look at it.

Comments

The first line of the example is a comment. Comments are remarks from the programmer inserted as reminders and to explain the actual source text. They are superfluous for the compiler, therefore the compiler ignores them.

But why bother writing something if the Java compiler ignores it? Well, comments are helpful for yourself, or maybe for colleagues and friends who want to read your source code. A source code without any comments at all is very hard and time consuming to understand, so you should get used to inserting short comments into each program at the right place. If you look into the source text a week or maybe a year later, comments will help you recollect what you had previously programmed.

Java has two kinds of comments. Shorter comments, which are accommodated on one line, are introduced with the string //. All characters between // and the end of the line are taken as comments.

```
// Hello World Program
import java.lang.*;

public class Hello World                      // Main class
   {
   public static void main(String[] args)     // main method
      {
      System.out.println("Hello World!");
      }
   }
```

You can create longer comments that extend over many lines by beginning each line with // or by typing the comment between the "brackets" /* and */ .

```
/* This is a
   comment
   extending over several lines */
```

The import statement

Let's jump to the second line. Here we are showing what we define as import statement:

```
import java.lang.*;
```

At first sight it looks really mysterious. Let's go back a bit so that we can find an explanation. Java is an object-oriented language, i.e. a substantial element in the program creation is the clustering of elements and activities that have to work with such data in defined logical units. These units are called *classes*.

This means that a Java program consists of a number of classes. When writing a new Java program, you will design some new classes and normally use several classes that were already available. The JDK has a lot of classes that can be used by a programmer. The programmer needs to import these classes into the program; the Java command for this is also logically called import.

Java packages

The classes enclosed with the JDK are not jumbled together but are subdivided into packages. The full class name consists of the package name and the actual class name. For instance, with java.lang.System.out: the package is java.lang and the class is System.out.

When importing, the full class name has to stand after the import statement; however, you often need several classes from a single package and therefore you usually have to import all classes from this package using the Joker character * for all classes; so, in the example, we have:

```
import java.lang.*;
```

With this, all classes are imported from the package java.lang and can be used in this program using their simple (actual) name.

When programming with Java, it is very helpful to know what is already contained in the packages and in their classes: you can insert these classes directly in your program, saving time and effort, assuming that you know how to program. Let's have a look at some commonly used packages:

- java.lang: very elementary classes are used either directly or indirectly by almost all the other Java classes. For this reason java.lang is imported at the beginning of any Java program, even if the programmer does not explicitly make it an import statement.[1]

- java.io: contains many useful classes for input and output with files.

- javax.swing and java.awt contain classes for creating windows and therefore a user interface.

> **NOTE**
>
> *You can find a full summary of all packages of the Java runtime library in the JDK-API specification. For this purpose, extract the ZIP file* j2sdk1_3_0-doc.zip *from the JDK directory of the accompanying CD, load the file* index.html *in your browser and click on the left* Java 2 Platform API Specification *(see also the section* Using the JDK documentation *in Chapter 6).*

Classes, methods and variables

As you already know, logically related data and operating activities are joined to the classes in Java. In this case, the data are described as a variable and the activities are described as methods (or also class functions).

Imagine that you need to write a Java program that controls a motor. This motor will have certain typical quantities (e.g. rotational speed, temperature) and activities such as start/stop motor, increase rotational speed, etc. In object-oriented programming, you can define just one class Motor that has

---

1. In the source text import java.lang.* is therefore unnecessary and you will not find this statement in many Java programs.

variables `rotational speed` and `temperature` as well as the methods `start()`, `stop()`, `increase_rotational speed()`. As source code, you would build this up as follows:

1 Draft the framework for the class `Motor` .

```
public class Motor
    {
    }
```

The definition of a class consists of the keywords `public`[2] `class` followed by the desired class name. Then there are some curly brackets `{}`. They mark the class segment, i.e. the "heart" of the class. Everything that is typed here belongs to this class.

2 Add the variables to the class.

```
public class Motor
    {
    float temperature;
    int   rotational seed;
    }
```

The declaration of a variable consists of the statement of a data type and a name. The data type tells the compiler which kind of data should be saved in the variables. In this example, temperature has to be managed as floating point number (`float`) and the rotational speed as integer number (`int`).

> **CAUTION**
>
> *Note that you need to insert a semicolon in the declaration after the variable name. The compiler requires a semicolon in order to recognise that a variable declaration has been completed.*

3 Add the methods to classes.

```
public class Motor
    {
    float temperature;
    int   rotational speed;

    start public void ()
      {
```

---

2. There are further additional remarks, such as `private` or `protected`, but we do not use them in this book.

```
    // here instructions to start
    }

stop public void ()
    {
    // here instructions to stop
    }

public void increase_rotational speed()
    {
    // here instructions to increase the rotational speed
    }
}
```

The definition of a method consists of several keywords (in the example above `public void`) followed by the name of the method with round brackets, such as `stop()`. As in the definition of the class segment, the name of the method is followed by two curly brackets in the method segment. All statements that are contained there build the statement block of the method.

The main() method

After this short review of classes and methods, we can now begin to analyse the program in the example.

After the `import` line you find the definition of a class name `HelloWorld`. You are already familiar with the concept. However, in the brackets, there is no variable declaration, but just the definition of a method with the name `main()`. This is a special method.

Each Java program must have a class that provides a special method called `public static void main(String[] args)`. The `main()` method is the first method that is called and worked on during the program execution (using the interpreter `java.exe`). We will consider further details (such as the meaning of `String[] args`) later.

Except for the unusual features discussed above, the `main()` method is quite normal. In its string you can insert statements that should be executed by calling `main()`. In our example, this is the line

`System.out.println("Hello World!");`

Here you can already see how the methods of a class are used in Java. `println()` itself is a method (of the class `System.out`) and in this line it is called by `main()`. Methods can therefore be called simultaneously. We will come back to this later.

Strings

Our program should welcome us with a warm "Hello World!". "Hello World!" is therefore the text to be output. So that the compiler knows that this sequence of characters is a text and not Java statements in the actual sense of the word, it appears in quotation marks as `"Hello World!"`.

`println()`

> **WHAT IS THIS?**
>
> *Portions of text, processed by the program, are defined* **as strings**. *Strings that can be found directly in the source code are put in quotation marks.*

In the example, the string `"Hello World!"` is submitted to the method `println()` as a parameter. It makes sure that the text appears in the console during the program execution.

The name of the source text file

You already know from the previous chapter that we saved the *HelloWorld* program under the name `HelloWorld.java`, with the same name as the class defined within it (with the ending `.java`). This cannot be a coincidence can it?

Indeed it is not. In Java there is a rule that the source code file should have exactly the same name as the class defined in it. Let's see what happens if we do not stick to this rule.

```
C:\Java_In_No_Time\HelloWorld>
C:\Java_In_No_Time\HelloWorld>
C:\Java_In_No_Time\HelloWorld>move HelloWorld.java HiWorld.java

C:\Java_In_No_Time\HelloWorld>javac HiWorld.java
HiWorld.java:4: class HelloWorld is public, should be declared in a file named H
elloWorld.java
public class HelloWorld
       ^
1 error

C:\Java_In_No_Time\HelloWorld>_
```

Figure 4.1: The file name and the class name do not agree.

In the console, change to the directory `c:\Java_In_No_Time\HelloWorld` and rename the file `HelloWorld.java` as `HiWorld.java`. You can also insert the command `move` for this:

```
move HelloWorld.java HiWorld.java
```

If you then start the Java compiler using `javac HiWorld.java` you will see that this does not like the Java compiler, so rename it to what it was called before.

But do any problems occur if you want to put two different classes in the same file? What should the file be called in this case?

The answer is simple: you can only define one class per file. If you want to write a program that consists of five files, you will distribute these classes between five files. [3]

In the last chapter, we recommended that you store each program in its own separate directory in order to avoid chaos on the hard disk. For example, we stored the program `HelloWorld` in a directory of the same name. You can call the class directory whatever you like, but it is recommended that the same name is given to the directory as the class name. [4]

Coding style

To conclude, a few more words about good and bad coding style.

Java's syntax is sometimes cryptic. Many meaningful syntactical elements are represented by single characters (such as {, (, ++, %), and individual syntactical elements can be combined in a variety of ways to create an outcome. In order to read and understand the source code it is necessary to adopt a certain writing style.

Here are some suggestions:

- If possible, write just one statement per line.
- Indent statement blocks.
- Use lots of blank characters and blank lines to break up the visual impact.

---

3. When you become a Java pro, you will learn that several classes can be saved in a single file (one `public`, the others without the name `public`). But, you will also understand why we have not explained the argument in this beginners' manual.
4. If you are an experienced Java programmer, the name of the directory can become important.

- Put comments in your code.

Make sure that your source texts do not look like the following:

```
import java.lang.*; public class HelloWorld
{public static void main(String[] args){
System.out.println("Hello World!");}}
```

Chapter 5

Numbers and text in Java programs

As you already know from the last chapter, a program processes data as variables. In this chapter we will look at this aspect more in detail. How are data represented? Where can the program store data at an intermediate level? What type of data are we talking about?

Variables and constants

Data can occur in two different forms in a program:

- as constants
- as variables.

Constants

We talk about constants if data are located directly in the source text. You have already learned about one kind of constant: the `String` constant.

```
// Hello World Program
import java.lang.*;

public class HelloWorld
  {
  public static void main(String[] args)
    {
    System.out.println("Hello World!");
    }
  }
```

`String` constants stand in double quotation marks by themselves. In addition to these, there are also number constants and single-character constants (the latter must stand in single quotation marks).

```
// constantexample
import java.lang.*;

public class constantexample
  {
  public static void main(String[] args)
    {
    // Stringconstant
    System.out.println("I am a Stringconstant");

    // Numberconstant
    System.out.println(3.1415);

    // Characterconstant
    System.out.println('C');
    }
  }
```

Variables

Constants are a wonderful thing, but they are not enough on their own to program properly. As well as constants, we need another option for storing data at intermediate level so that we can access the data at any time and change them if necessary. Variables offer this option.

To become more familiar with the concept and the working of variables, we can think of them as drawers. So, you start out with a cupboard with hundreds of unused drawers. If you want to save a number or any other kind of data – let's assume, for instance, that you are breeding rabbits and you want to keep a stock of them – look for an unused drawer, open it and write the number of rabbits on the bottom of the drawer. In order to always know in which drawer the number of the rabbit has been stored, choose a name for the drawer, such as `rabbits`, and write it on the front of the drawer. If, in the future, you want to know how many rabbits you have, simply go to the cupboard, open the drawer caled `rabbits` and read the number. If the number of rabbits has changed, open the drawer, delete the previous value and write in the new value.

Figure 5.1: Variables are, like drawers, intermediate memory.

Of course, in programming, there are no cupboard drawers, but rather a working memory. When you declare a variable in a program, the compiler makes sure that during the execution of the program, some place is reserved for this variable in the working memory. After this, you can save values in the variable, and query the current value of the variables. But how do we declare a variable?

Declaring variables

Each variable declaration consists of the output of the data type of the variables and of the variable name, for instance

```
int myvar;
```

- The data type informs the compiler which kind of data are stored, and how much memory is needed.
- The name of the variables should be clear. Remember that Java distinguishes between capitalization and lower case.

But, one step at a time.

1 Begin a new program, i.e. create a new subdirectory *variable declaration* in the *Java_In_No_Time* directory and start an editor (such as Notepad).

2 Draft the program framework in the editor:

```
// Demo for variable declaration
import java.lang.*;

public class variable_declaration
```

```
    {
    public static void main(String[] args)
      {

      }
    }
```

3 At the beginning of the method segment of `main()` indicate the data type and the name of the variables that have to be set up.

```
// Demo for variable declaration
import java.lang.*;

public class variable_declaration
    {
    public static void main(String[] args)
      {
      int my Var;
      }
    }
```

The data type (`int` in our example) tells the Java compiler which data need to be included in the variable. In the variables `int` you can include, for instance, integer numbers. We will look at further types of data below.

You can choose the name of the variables (`myVar` in the example) as long as you keep to some rules:

- The variable name must begin with a letter and cannot contain any blanks or special characters. Umlauts are not accepted.

- The name should not be too long, but it should be meaningful so that you can tell the use of the variable from its name.

- It is frequently difficult to find meaningful names for dummy variables that are used only for a short time to save intermediate results. Many programmers name them simply `i`, `j`, `tmp` or something similar.

- Finally, the variable name needs to be unambiguous, i.e. you are not allowed to give two variables the same name.

CAUTION

Do not forget that you must type a semicolon at the end of the variable declaration. We learnt about the semicolon requirement at the beginning of this book. In Java, variable declarations and statements must always be closed with a semicolon.

The data type – variables for any purpose

There is some more important information about data types that you should know. As we have already mentioned, in Java, every variable declaration begins with a type statement, which shows the compiler the kind of data that can be saved in the variable.

We could just accept this statement and continue to look at the different data types that are available. However, it is interesting to analyse why the compiler actually needs the type statement. If you want to learn more, then read about working memory in the next section in this book, where we look at all the other types of Java.

The meaning of the data type

The compiler reserves space in the working memory for every variable that you declare in your program.[1] If you assign the variables a value in the course of the program, then the compiler files this value in the memory. If you query the value of the variables, then the compiler reads the value from the memory of the variables.

So far, everything seems easy. Things become complex when the working memory of the computer is an electronic, digital memory consisting of thousands of cells that can save just 1 (voltage in) or 0 (voltage out). You can simulate this memory yourself.

---

1. The compiler does not reserve the working memory directly. It is more correct to say that the compiler creates the machine code that reserves the working memory during the execution of the program.

Take a piece of graph paper, draw a frame around about 20 by 10 boxes, try to imagine that in each box you can only write 1 or a 0 , and your working memory is ready (Figure 5.1).

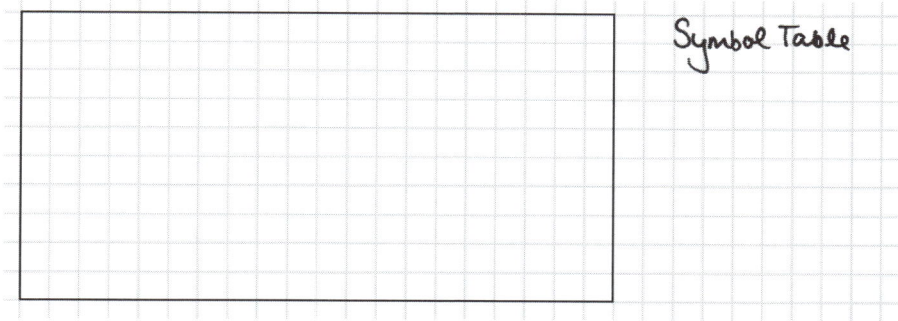

Symbol Table

Figure 5.1: Simulating digital memory.

Let's assume that you declare a variable var1. Since you can save only zeros and ones in the working memory, you need to convert the number 3 into a series of zeros and ones, a so-called binary representation. In the binary system the binary number 11 is derived from the decimal number 3 (1x2 + 1x1).

> **NOTE**
>
> *A binary number is expressed as the sum of powers of 2 (1, 2, 4, 8, 16, etc.) (rather than as the sum of powers of 10, as we are used to with our decimal numbers).*

You can now reserve the first two cells in your simulated working memory for the variable var1 and insert the number 11. But what if you want to insert the value 5 in var1 later? The value 5, like 101, is binary and needs three memory cells. However, for our variable, only two memory cells are reserved, and the compiler cannot extend the storage of a variable that has already been reserved. We must reserve enough memory cells directly in the declaration of the variables. Let's be generous and reserve 16 cells for var1.

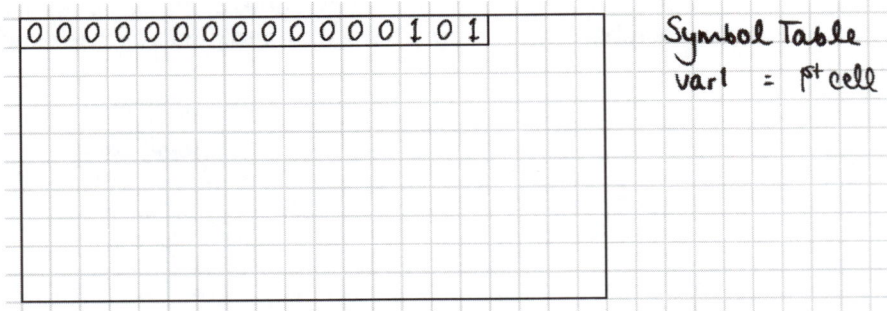

0 0 0 0 0 0 0 0 0 0 0 0 1 0 1

Symbol Table
var1 = 1st cell

Figure 5.2: Reserving 16 memory cells for var1 *in the simulated memory.*

WHAT IS THIS?

Programmers count memory cells in bits and bytes. A bit is an information unit that can adopt either the value 1 or 0. The binary number 101 therefore consists of three bits. In the working memory, each memory cell can save exactly 1 bit of information. One byte corresponds to 8 bits.

16 memory cells (= 16 bits) therefore correspond to 2 bytes. If we establish that the first memory cell determines the plus or the minus sign (0 for positive, 1 for negative numbers), 15 bits remain for the actual value – this means that now we can store values between -32.768 and +32.767 in var1.

Then we want to store a fractional number with a fractional digit (in programming jargon, this is called the "floating point number"). We declare a new variable var2 and reserve the next 2 bytes in our simulated working memory for it (Figure 5.3). We now want to save the value 1,3 in the variable.

How should we code the number 1,3 as a bit sequence? Should we convert 1 and 3 into binary numbers and then arrange them so that the value is put in front of the comma in the first byte, and the value in the second byte is put after the comma? In this case, we could only save small numbers with very few fractional digits in 2 bytes. It is better to print out the number in exponential notation, and then redraft it so that a 0 stands in front of the comma. Therefore, at first $1,3 \times 10^0$ will be derived from 1,3 and then $0,13 \times 10^1$.

Rather than 2 bytes, we use 4 bytes for the floating point variable. In the first three bytes, we save the fractional digits (13 = 1101) – we do not need the zero since we convert all floating point numbers so that they begin with a zero before the comma. In the fourth byte, we save a base to the power of 10 (1 in our example).

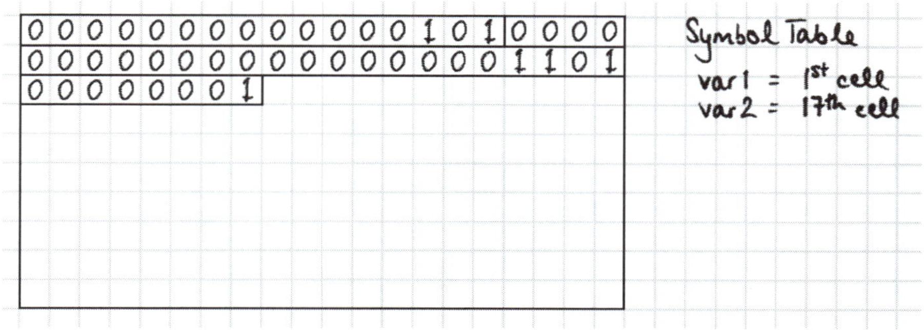

0 0 0 0 0 0 0 0 0 0 0 0 1 0 1 0 0 0 0	Symbol Table
0 0 0 0 0 0 0 0 0 0 0 0 0 0 1 1 0 1	var1 = 1st cell
0 0 0 0 0 0 1	var2 = 17th cell

Figure 5.3: Adding memory cells for var2.

To conclude, we also reserve a variable var3, to which we want to give the character C. Characters are coded using the ASCII table. In this table, each character is given a number value. In order to give the character C in the memory, we reserve 1 byte of memory; look at the ASCII table (see Appendix D) to see what code value the capital letter C has, and convert it into binary code (67 = 0100 0011), which we save in the variable (Figure 5.4).

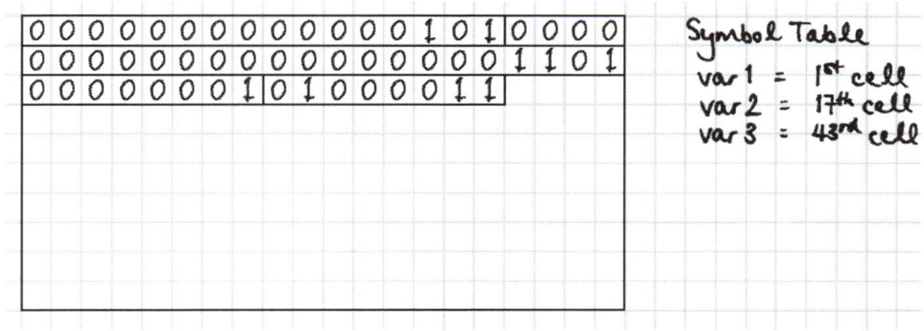

0 0 0 0 0 0 0 0 0 0 0 0 1 0 1 0 0 0 0	Symbol Table
0 0 0 0 0 0 0 0 0 0 0 0 0 0 1 1 0 1	var1 = 1st cell
0 0 0 0 0 0 0 1 0 1 0 0 0 0 1 1	var2 = 17th cell
	var3 = 43rd cell

Figure 5.4: Adding memory cells for var3.

Now we have reserved memory for the variables of three different data types (integer numbers, floating point numbers and characters). We know that each data type has a specific memory requirement and its own coding method. Therefore, the compiler uses the type statement for each variable declaration. From this, the compiler can tell:

- how much memory it needs to reserve for the variable;
- how it is to code the values (which are assigned to the variables) into bit sequences, and give them in the memory area of the variables (and the reverse; when querying the value of the variable, the bit sequence is changed back into a value).

> **NOTE**
>
> *The coding methods introduced in this section for integer numbers, floating point numbers and characters are simplified versions of the codings that run in the computer.*

To conclude, we need to point out that the compiler also uses the type statement to guarantee the correct use of the variables. Therefore, the compiler must create another byte code for the division of two integer numbers – as well as for the division of two floating point numbers – it does not allow the division of two strings.

Java data types

In Java, there are two different categories of data types:

- elementary data types
- defined data types

The elementary data types are firmly anchored in the language. Each data type has its own keyword, which you give as a type in the variable declaration.

If you want to set up a variable, for instance, in which you wish to save integer numbers, give `int` as a data type:

```
int mynumber;
```

For instance, when you you want to store a particularly high integer number, the storage the compiler reserves for the `int`-variables may not be enough. In this case, to be sure, declare the variable as `long`:

```
long mynumber;
```

The most important elementary data types are listed in Table 5.1. For each data type, it is specified which kind of data you can store in the variables of the respective data type.

Data type	Domains[2]
Boolean	Truth values: true, false
Char	Single character: a, !, \n
Int	Integer numbers between −2 147 483 648 and 2 147 483 647
Long	Integer numbers between −9 223 372 036 854 775 808 and 9 223 372 036 854 775 807
Float	Floating-point numbers between −3.40e+38 and +3.40e+38
Double	Floating-point numbers between −1.79e+308 and +1.79e+308

Table 5.1: The most important elementary data types.

If these data types are not enough, you need to use self-defined data types. The mechanism to adopt here is the definition of a suitable class. These data types are also called class types. In this book, you will learn about them in more detail.

In Java packages, there is a variety of these classes. An example is the class `String` (`java.lang` package), which is used for more comfortable use of the character strings. In order to declare a `String` variable, proceed as you usually do when declaring the variable of an elementary data type. First comes the type statement, and then the variable name:

```
String myString;
```

WHAT IS THIS?

The variables of class types are called instances or objects (for further details, see Chapter 12).

---

2. The domains given are minimum domains dictated by the C++ standard. Depending on the operating systems and compiler used, more extended domains are also possible. So, the domain for `int` in the Visual C++ compiler is as large as the domain of the data type `lang`.

Saving values in variables

We have talked a lot about storing values in the variables. Now we will put it into practice:

1 Begin a new program, i.e. create a new subdirectory `variable assignment` in the directory `Java_In_No_Time` and start an editor (e.g. Notepad).

2 Draft the program framework.

```
// example for variable assignment
import java.lang.*;

public class variable_assignment
    {
    public static void main(String[] args)
      {
      }
    }
```

3 Define an `int`, `double` and a `string` variable.

```
// example for  variable assignment
import java.lang.*;

public class variable_assignment
    {
    public static void main(String[] args)
      {
      int     number;
      double  fractional_number;
      String str;
      }
    }
```

4 Assign a suitable value to the variables. This is possible by means of the output of the variables following = and the value:

```
// example for  variable assignment
import java.lang.*;

public class variable_assignment
    {
    public static void main(String[] args)
      {
      int     number;
      double fractional_number;
      String str;

      number = 124;
     fractional_number= 3.1415;
      str = "This is a character string";
      }
    }
```

> **CAUTION**
>
> *The type of variable must be suitable for the variables. Therefore you cannot assign an integer number to a* string *variable.*
>
> *Remember that, in decimal numbers, you must type a point (e.g.* 3.1415 *and not* 3,1415*).*

Initialising variables in the definition

If you want, you can also assign an initial value to a variable directly in the declaration:

```
int number    = 100;
double fractional_number = 333.33;
string str        = "Hello";
```

> **CAUTION**
>
> *When inputting decimal numbers, you must insert a decimal point instead of the comma (the same happens in pocket calculators).*

Querying the values of the variables

It is worth saving a value in a variable only if you want to access the value of the variables again at a later stage.

The following list continues from the example of the previous section, and queries the values of the declared variables in order to check them before outputting them.

5 Question the values of the variables and issue them.

```
// example for  variable assignment (continuation)
import java.lang.*;

public class variable_assignment
    {
    public static void main(String[] args)
        {
        int     number;
        double  fractional_number;
```

```
        String str;

        number= 124;
        fractional_number= 3.1415;
        str = "This is a character string";

        System.out.println(number);
        System.out.println(fractional_number);
        System.out.println(str);
        }
    }
```

6 Save the program in the directory c:\Java_In_No_Time\variable assignment under the name variable_assignment.java.

7 Change to this directory in the console, compile and start the program.

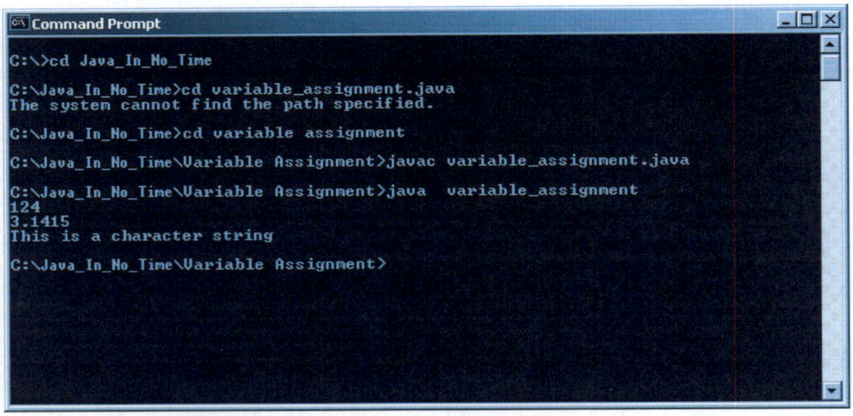

Figure 5.5: Output of the variable assignment *program.*

Obviously, you can assign a new value to the variable using the variable name, and query the current value of the variable. But how can the compiler know, when it comes across a variable name, whether it needs to assign a value to the variable or query the actual value of the variables?

Quite simple!

- If the variable name appears on the left of an assignment (as in number = 124;), the compiler assigns the value of the expression on the right of the equals sign (in programming languages this is also described as the = operator).

- If the variable name appears at any other place (such as in `System.out.println(number);`), the compiler substitutes the variable name with the current value of the variable.

Let's look at another example of queries and assignments.

Simultaneous queries and assignments

If two variables of the same data type are available, you can assign the value of one of them to the other.

```
import java.lang.*;

public class variable_assignment
    {
    public static void main(String[] args)
        {
        int   number1;
        int   number2;

        number1 = 11;
        number2 = number1;
        }
    }
```

First, pay attention to the line

```
number2 = number1;
```

Here, the compiler substitutes the variable name `number1` with the current value of this variable (i.e. `11`) and assigns it to the variable `number2`. The value 11 stands in both variables `number1` and `number2` after this statement.

> **NOTE**
>
> *If you declare several variables of a data type, you only have to give the data type once and then the single variables after this, separated by commas.*
>
> ```
> int number1, number2;
> ```

We can even question the value of a variable in a statement, modify it and assign it to the variable again:

```
int   number = 11;

number = number * 3;
```

Here, the variable `number` is declared and initialised with the value 11. This becomes interesting in the statement

```
number = number * 3;
```

When evaluating this statement, the compiler begins on the right side of the = operator. It substitutes `number` with the current value of the variable (11). It multiplies this value by 3. It saves the result (33) as the new value of `number`.

Chapter 6

Working with numbers and text

So far, our example programs have been neither particularly useful nor really exciting because we had not learned yet how to reprocess the data that are saved in the variables.

Calculations

In addition to the assignment of values to the variables, there are further operations that can be carried out on data. The data type establishes which operations can be used. For instance, you can add, subtract, divide and multiply numbers:

```
// multiplication
import java.lang.*;

public class multiplication
    {
    public static void main(String[] args)
        {
        int n_1, n_2;

        n_1 = 10;
        n_2 = n_1;

        n_1 = n_1 * n_2;

        System.out.println("the result is" + n_1);
        }
    }
```

the output is:[1]

```
the result is 100
```

As you can see, the multiplication was carried out using the * character multiplication operator. Java has a series of further operators to manipulate numbers (see Table 6.1).

---

1. Note that for the output with `System.out.println` the output string has been combined with the value of the variable `n_1` with +. We will go into more detail about this later.

Operator	Meaning	Example
=	Assignment	`var = 3;`
+	Addition	`var = 3 + 4;     // var = 7;`
−	Subtraction	`var = 3 - 4;     // var = -1;`
+ / −	Plus or minus sign	`var =   - 4;     // var = -4;`
*	Multiplication	`var = 3 * 4;     // var = 12;`

/	Division	`var = 3 / 4;     // var = 0;`
		`var = 3.0/4.0;   // var = 0.75;`

%	Modulus (integer remainder of a division of integer numbers)	`var = 3 % 4;     // var = 3;`

Table 6.1: The arithmetic operators.

> **CAUTION**
>
> *Note that the modulus operation can only be applied to integer numbers (`int` or `long`), while division provides different results for integer numbers and floating-point numbers. During the division of floating-point numbers, the operator returns the exact result; in the division of integer numbers, it returns an integral result. This means that the fractional part is simply rejected.*

Calculating mathematical formulae

Using the operators introduced above, you can calculate simple formulae.

Imagine you want to go on holiday to Arizona. You read on the Internet that in Arizona it is 20 degrees Fahrenheit at the moment. But what is this temperature in centigrade?

The formula for the conversion of Fahrenheit to centigrade is as follows:

```
centigrade = (fahrenheit - 32) * 5 / 9
```

Let's now create a program that calculates how warm 20 degrees Fahrenheit really is using this formula.

1 Begin a new program, i.e. insert a new subdirectory *fahrenheit* into the directory *Java_In_No_Time* and start an editor (e.g. notepad).

2 Draft the program framework.

```
// fahrenheit conversion
import java.lang.*;

public class fahrenheit
    {
    public static void main(String[] args)
        {

        }
    }
```

3 Declare two `double` variables for the temperature in Fahrenheit and centigrade.

```
// fahrenheit conversion
import java.lang.*;

public class fahrenheit
    {
    public static void main(String[] args)
        {
        double fahrenheit;
        double centigrade;
        }
    }
```

For the variable `fahrenheit` we select the data type `double` so that we can also calculate values with a decimal place (for example 20.5).

For the variable `centigrade` we select the data type `double` because the result of the formula usually gives a number with a decimal place because of the multiplication with `5/9`.

4 Initialise the variable `fahrenheit`.

```
// fahrenheit conversion
import java.lang.*;

public class fahrenheit
    {
    public static void main(String[] args)
```

```
      {
      double fahrenheit;
      double centigrade;
      fahrenheit = 20;
      }
   }
```

5 Add the formula for the conversion to centigrade.

```
// fahrenheit conversion
import java.lang.*;

public class fahrenheit
   {
   public static void main(String[] args)
      {
      double fahrenheit;
      double centigrade;

      fahrenheit = 20;

      centigrade = fahrenheit - 32 * 5.0 / 9.0;
      }
   }
```

Why write 5.0/9.0 instead of 5/9 in this formula?

5/9 is an integer division that the compiler would calculate to 0, since it simply cuts off the fractional digits.

5.0/9.0, on the other hand, is a floating-point number division that the compiler calculates, as required, to 0.55555555.

We have not yet dealt with all the traps though.

Bracketing expressions

In maths, and in Java, the calculation of lines follows the calculation of dots. The above expression is not calculated as

```
(fahrenheit - 32) * 5.0/9.0
```

but as

```
fahrenheit - (32 * 5.0/9.0)
```

In order for the compiler to evaluate the individual operators in the desired order, we need to insert brackets – just as we do in maths.

6 Insert brackets in order to guarantee the correct order of the operators.

```
// fahrenheit conversion
import java.lang.*;

public class fahrenheit
    {
    public static void main(String[] args)
        {
        double fahrenheit;
        double centigrade;

        fahrenheit = 20;

        centigrade = (fahrenheit - 32) * 5.0 / 9.0;
        }
    }
```

7 Output the result of the calculations.

```
// fahrenheit conversion
import java.lang.*;

public class fahrenheit
    {
    public static void main(String[] args)
        {
        double fahrenheit;
        double centigrade;

        fahrenheit = 20;

        centigrade = (fahrenheit - 32) * 5.0 / 9.0;

        System.out.println(fahrenheit +
                " correspond to degree fahrenheit ");
        System.out.println(centigrade +
                " degree centigrade");
        }
    }
```

8 Save the program as c:\Java_In_No_Time\fahrenheit \fahrenheit.java. Compile the program and execute it (Figure 6.1).

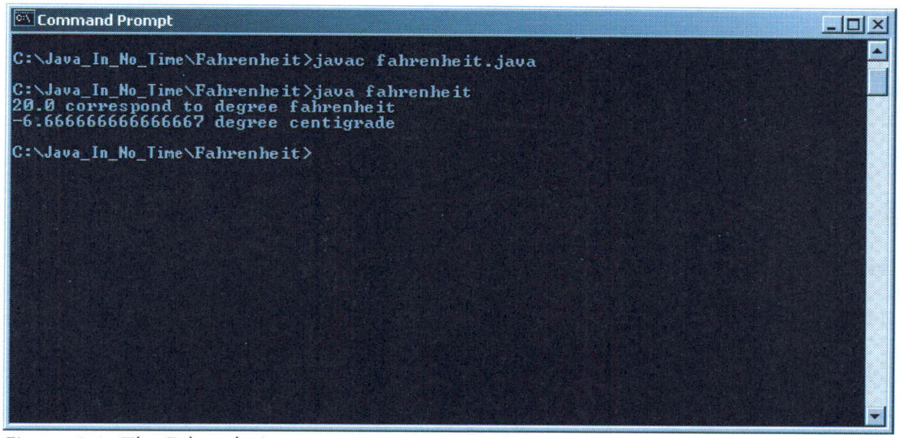

Figure 6.1: The Fahrenheit *program.*

Mathematical functions

Certain frequently used mathematical functions, such as the calculation of a square root, or the calculation of the sine of an angle, can be converted by means of the basic arithmetical operations, but only with some difficulty. For the most important of these calculations, there is the class `Math` in the package `java.lang`, which provides the so-called static[2] methods. Table 6.2 shows a selection of the most important ones:

---

2. This is not important in the context of our book. We only mention it so that you will recognise the concept.

Method	Description
`Math.acos(x)`	Arcus cosine of x
`Math.asin(x)`	Arcus cosine of x
`Math.atan(x)`	Arcus tangent of x
`Math.cos(x)`	Cosine of x
`Math.cosh(x)`	Cosine hyperbolic of x
`Math.sin(x)`	Sine hyperbolic of x
`Math.sinh(x)`	Sine hyperbolic of x
`tan(x)`	Tangent of x
`tanh(x)`	Tangent hyperbolic of x
`Math.abs(x)`	Absolute amount of x
`Math.floor(x)`	High integer number that is lower than or equal to the value submitted
`Math.ceil(x)`	The lowest integer number that is higher than or equal to the value submitted
`Math.round(x)`	Rounds up x to the next integer number above or below
`Math.exp(x)`	Exponential function (i.e. high x)
`Math.log(x)`	Natural logarithm (i.e. on base e)
`pow(x,y)`	Raises the number x to the power of y
`sqrt(x)`	Square root of x

Table 6.2: The mathematical functions of the class `Math`.

Programming with these methods is very simple: you call the methods with their name, submit the necessary parameter to them and the result is returned. For example, to calculate the square root of 102355, write:

```
double root;     // variable for the inclusion of the result
root = Math.sqrt(102355);
```

But how can you know what a method does, which parameters it needs and which result it returns?

Either you look for a good manual in which the single functions (as well as the other elements of the Java package) are introduced, or you look in the documentation installed with the JDK. You can find the HTML file *index.html* (which you can open with a Web browser) in the subdirectory *docs\api* during the installation in the directory *c:\jdk1.3*.

Using the JDK documentation

The JDK documentation contains extensive instructions for both beginners and professionals about the Java package, its classes and methods.

> **NOTE**
>
> *You can find the JDK documentation on the Internet on the Java Web site http://java.sun.com. You can also find the documentation about the Version 1.3 in the JDK directory on the accompanying CD. It is contained in the ZIP file j2sdk1_3_0-doc.zip and can be unpacked with every current ZIP program, for example Win Zip. (Make sure that the path details are followed during the unpacking.) The documentation itself is available in HTML format and can be viewed using a browser (e.g. Internet Explorer, Netscape Navigator).*

Let's assume that you want to set up a square root in your program. You can vaguely remember that there is a class `Math`, but you have forgotten the exact method name. Using your browser, call the `index.html` file of the JDK documentation (if you have unpacked the files from the ZIP file into *C:* you can find the `index.html` file under `c:\jdk1.3\docs\index.html`) (Figure 6.2).

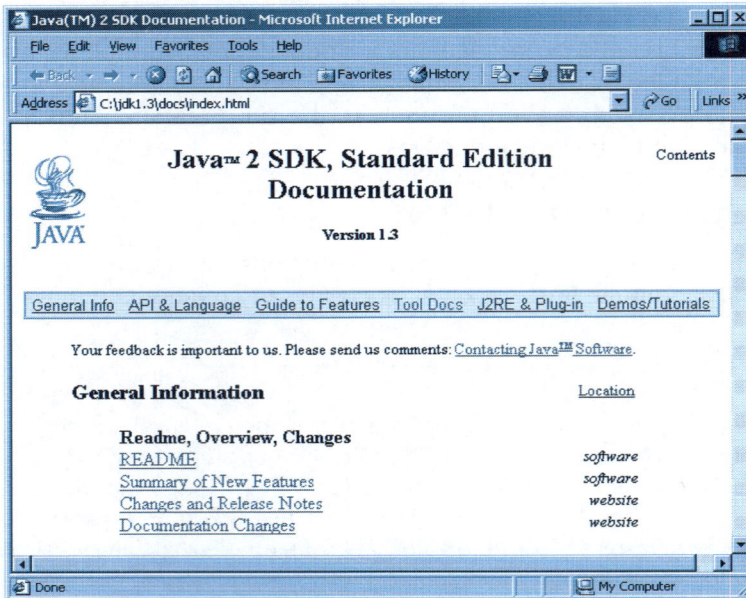

Figure 6.2: Java documentation.

The page contains extensive references. To look up the Java classes select the link *Java 2 Platform API Specification* at the bottom of the page, which takes you to a page where you can look through both class package names. The search for `Math` quickly produces the page with all the methods of this class. There you also find the method with the required functionality: `sqrt()` (Figure 6.3).

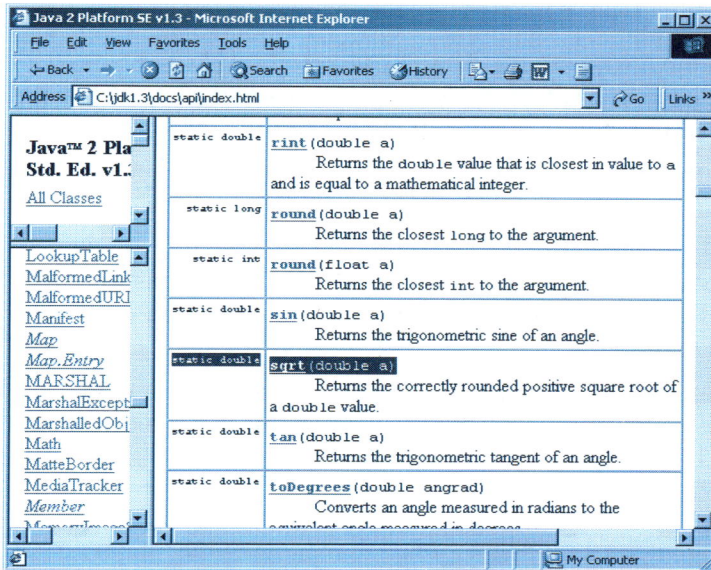

Figure 6.3: The elements of the class `Math`.

From the documentation, you gather that `sqrt()` expects a `double` value as parameter. The first column shows that a result of type `double` is returned. (By the way, the additional remark `static` means that this method can be called even if no instance of `Math` has been created. We will look at this again in a later chapter.)

But what should you do if you are looking for a particular functionality but do not remember the name of the affiliated class? This is just bad luck. There is nothing else you can do apart from leaf through the packages and, if necessary, read all the classes listed. Maybe you will find a class or method that provides exactly what you need. Maybe you will find nothing and will have to create your own class. However, by going through these packages you will learn lots of classes and, when facing the next problem, you will already know that there is a class that provides what you require.

TIP

Rummage through the JDK documentation. Leaf through the different packages and their classes and methods. Let yourself be inspired and discover what you can do with the classes provided.

Type strictness and type conversion

Before we look in the next section at how to use a method like `Math.sqrt()` in a program, we have to have a brief look at the meaning of the data types of the parameter and of the result value of the function.

Let's begin with the parameter of the `Math.sqrt()` method. In the JDK documentation we have seen that this parameter is of the type `double`. What does this mean?

Java is a very type-sensitive programming language. This means that if the compiler requires a specific value at a specific place, you can only use a value of this type there.

The type `double` stands for all real numbers (as long as you are working in the domain of the data type; see Table 5.1). This means that we can submit the constants -3.14 or 2.0 or a `double` variable as arguments:

```
double value = 0.575;
double result1, result2, result3;
result1 = Math.sqrt( 3.14 );
result2 = Math.sqrt( 2.0 );
result3 = Math.sqrt(value);
```

Can we also submit the whole number 2?

```
result1 = Math.sqrt( 2 );       // is this correct?
```

At first glance we would say: "Of course, 2 is definitely a real number".

But be careful: the Java compiler here is fussy. It considers the constant 2 as an integer number, i.e. of the type `int` (unlike the constant 2.0, which is of the type `double`). Therefore, we are dealing with different types, and the compiler should actually quit the call `Math.sqrt(2)` with an error message.

If the compiler does not give any error message, this is because it cannot convert a type into another automatically for certain type combinations. This happens, for instance, in the conversion of `int` into `long` or of `float` into `double` or even for the conversion of an integer number (`int` or `long`) into a floating-point number (`float` or `double`).

And how does the result appear? The function `double Math.sqrt(double x)` returns the root calculated as a value of the type `double`. We can save this value in a `float` or `double` variable:

```
double result;

result = Math.sqrt(0.54);
```

What happens if we want to save the result in a `long` variable?

```
long result;

result = Math.sqrt(0.54);
```

The compiler cannot then execute an automatic conversion. Think about it: it is a different thing converting an integer into a floating-point number than converting a floating-point number into an integer.

For the compiler, it is no more difficult to get a floating-point number from any other integer number than for you to get 2.0 from 2. But not every floating-point number can be converted into an integer number so easily. Most floating-point numbers have fractional digits or a value that does lie outside of the value range of `long` data types. The conversion of these floating-point numbers into integer numbers would not be possible without loss of data. Therefore, the compiler does not carry out an automatic type conversion.

The above attempt to assign the `double` result of the function to a `long` variable will lead to an error message from the compiler. Try it again. Draft a simple program and insert the statements

```
long result;

result = Math.sqrt(0.54);
```

and compile.

Sometimes, you want to carry out a type conversion (also called cast). You can put the desired data type before the value that is to be converted:

```
long result;
result = (long) Math.sqrt(0.54);
```

This statement tells the compiler:

"I am aware that you do not actually accept any conversion of `double` values into `long` values and that a data loss could occur, but in this case the value is not too high and the fractional digits are of not interest to me. I therefore take on full responsibility; so, get on with it and please save the value in a `long` variable."

In the variable `result` the value 0 is saved, instead of the correct value `0.7348` (= root from 0.54).

> **CAUTION**
>
> *The explicit type conversion is not possible for every type combination, but only for those conversions that are supported by the compiler. For example, you cannot convert strings that contain numbers (for example "312") into an int value with an explicit conversion. In order to convert strings into numbers, in Java there are special methods, which you will learn later.*

Using trigonometric methods

If you work with trigonometric methods, you must take into account that they always require values in radian measures as parameters. In the radian measure, the angle is expressed not in degrees, but as the length of the arch that cuts out the angle from the circle (complete perimeter 2π): $1° = 360°/2\pi$; 1 rad = $2\pi/360°$.

Assume that you want to determine the height of a building. You place yourself some distance in front of the building and mark this point on the ground. From this point, you take a bearing off the edge of the roof, and measure the angle between the plotted line to the edge of the roof and the ground – we'll say 25 degrees. Now you have to measure the distance from the building – we'll say 18 metres. According to the formula

```
h = distance * tan a
```

we can now calculate the height (Figure 6.4).

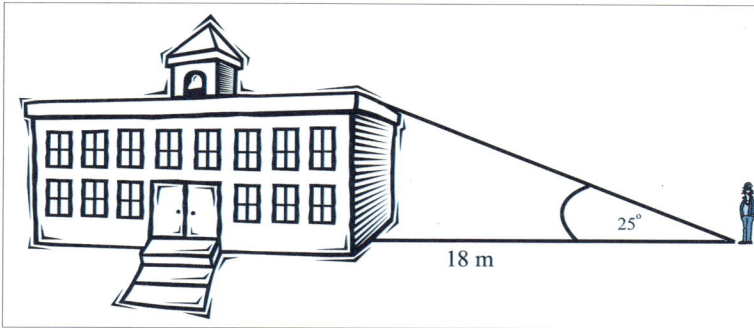

Figure 6.4: Calculating the height of a building.

1 Begin a new program, i.e. create a new subdirectory *Building height* in the directory *Java_In_No_Time* and start an editor (e.g. Notepad).

2 Draft the program framework.

```
// Calculate the height of the building
import java.lang.*;

public class Buildingheight
   {
   public static void main(String[] args)
      {
      }
   }
```

3 Declare and initialise the variable for the angle measured, the distance from the wall of the building, and the height that is to be calculated.

```
// Calculate the height of the building
import java.lang.*;

public class Buildingheight
   {
   public static void main(String[] args)
      {
      double angle = 25.0; // angle (in degrees)
      double distance = 18.0; // distance (in m)
      double height;
      }
   }
```

4 Convert the angle from degrees to rad.

```
// Calculate the height of the building
import java.lang.*;

public class Buildingheight
   {
```

```
public static void main(String[] args)
  {
  double angle= 25.0; // angle direction line-ground
                      // (in degree)
  double distance = 18.0; // distance
                          // direction point - building  wall
  double height;

  angle = angle* 2 * 3.14159 / 360;
  }
}
```

5 Call the method `Math.tan()` in order to calculate the building height.

```
// calculate the Buildingheight
import java.lang.*;

public class Buildingheight
  {
  public static void main(String[] args)
    {
    double angle = 25.0; // angle direction line-ground
                         // (in degrees)
    double distance = 18.0; // distance
                            // direction point - building  wall
    double height;

    angle = angle * 2 * 3.14159 / 360;
    height = distance * Math.tan(angle);
    }
  }
```

6 Output the result.

```
// calculate the Buildingheight
import java.lang.*;

public class Buildingheight
  {
  public static void main(String[] args)
    {
    double angle = 25.0; // angle direction line-ground
                         // (in degrees)
    double distance = 18.0; // distance
                            // direction point - building wall
    double height;

    angle = angle * 2 * 3.14159 / 360;
    height = distance * Math.tan (angle);

    System.out.println("The building is "
                       + height + " m high" );
    }
  }
```

7 Save the program in the directory `c:\Java_In_No_Time\ Buildingheight` as `Buildingheight.java`. In the console, change to `c:\Java_In_No_Time\Buildin#gheight` and compile the program. Then execute it (Figure 6.5).

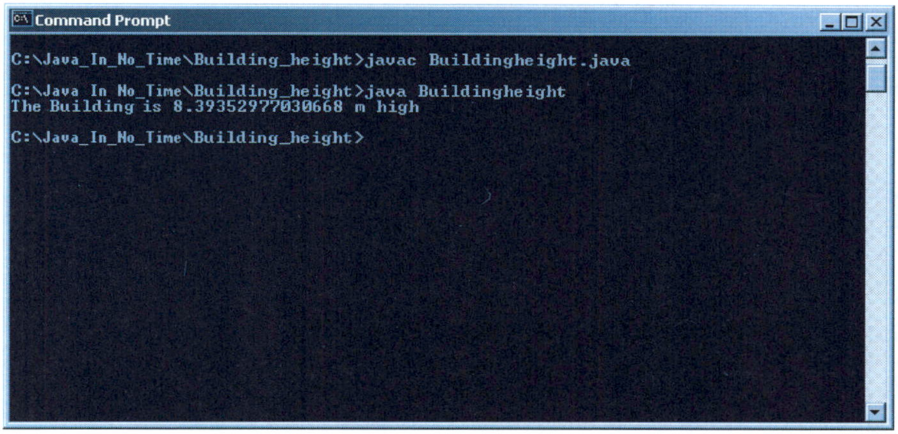

Figure 6.5: Output of the calculated building height.

Other counters

We cannot move on from the topic of numbers and operators without taking a look at some important shortened forms for assignments.

Combined assignments

Until now, in order to change the value of a variable (let's say multiply it by 3), you would have written:

```
int var = 12;

var = var * 3; // or also: var = 3 * var;
```

For this purpose, there is a shortened form based on the use of the combined `*=` operators:

```
int var = 12;

var *= 3;
```

To begin with, you need to get used to this shortened form, but it will save you a lot of typing.

Combined assignment operators are available for all arithmetical operations: `+=, -=, *=, /=, %=`.

Increment and decrement

Two of the most used operations in programming are the increase and decrease of an integer variable by 1 (see Chapter 9). For this purpose there are two special operators in Java: ++ and --.

The statement

```
var++; // or: ++var;
```

increases the value of the variable `var` by 1.

> **WHAT IS THIS?**
>
> *The increase by 1 is described as* increment.

The statement

```
var--; // or: --var;
```

decreases the value of the variable `var` by 1.

> **WHAT IS THIS?**
>
> *The reduction by 1 is described as* decrement.

What is special about the operators ++ and -- is that you can also use them in expressions (therefore on the right side of the assignment):

```
var1 = 3 * var2++;
```

and that you can put them both before and after the name of the variable:

```
++var;
```

```
var++;
```

To explain the options and traps that accompany these notations would be going too far at this point (apart from which, there are more traps than options). You can avoid the traps if you only use the operators with the name of the variables alone (and not in expressions in which other operators are used).

Working with strings

In Chapter 5 we pointed out that in Java there is no built-in data type for strings, but a class `String` defined in the package `java.lang` in which strings can be saved.

Defining and assigning string variables

At first glance, you work with the class type `String` in the same way as with the elementary data type. Let's give an example.

1 Begin a new program, i.e. create a new subdirectory, *StringDemo,* in the directory *Java_In_No_Time* and start an editor (e.g. notepad).

2 Draft the program framework.

```
// StringDemo
import java.lang.*;

public class StringDemo
   {
   public static void main(String[] args)
      {
      }
   }
```

3 Declare a variable of the type `String` and assign it the character string `"My name is Dirk"`.

```
// StringDemo
import java.lang.*;

public class StringDemo
   {
   public static void main(String[] args)
      {
      String myname;
      myname = "My name is Jonathan";
      }
   }
```

4 Output the string on the screen.

```
// StringDemo
import java.lang.*;

public class StringDemo
   {
   public static void main(String[] args)
      {
```

```
    String myname;
    myname = "My name is Jonathan";
    System.out.println(myName);
    }
}
```

5 Save the program in the directory `c:\Java_In_No_Time\StringDemo` as `StringDemo.java`. In the console, change to `c:\Java_In_No_Time\StringDemo` and compile the program. Then execute it.

Adding strings to other strings

An important operation in the processing of strings is adding one string to another.

WHAT IS THIS?

The process of adding strings together plays such an important role in programming and in theoretical computer science that there is a name for it: concatenation.

In order to make this addition of strings as easy as possible, the class `String` has been implemented so that strings can be added to each other with the + operator. You have already seen this in some previous examples.

Let's look at it more in detail. Because you have mastered the first fundamental step in the creation of a program, from now on the elementary steps will be kept short and sweet.

1 Begin a new program and draft the program framework.

```
// concatenation of strings
import java.lang.*;

public class StringDemo2
   {
   public static void main(String[] args)
      {
      }
   }
```

2 Declare three string variables: one that you initialize directly with a welcome note, one that you initialize with a name, and one for the combined string.

```
// concatenation of strings
import java.lang.*;

public class stringdemo2
   {
  public static void main(string[] args)
     {
     String welcoming_word  = "Hello";
     String name     = "Paul Watkinson";
     String output;
     }
   }
```

3 Add the welcome note and the name to each other and assign the result to the string variable output.

```
// concatenation of strings
import java.lang.*;

public class stringdemo2
   {
 public static void main(string[] args)
     {
     string welcoming word  = "Hello";
     string name    = "Paul Watkinson";
     string output;

     output = welcoming_word + " " + name + "!";
       }
   }
```

In order to avoid the name from sticking directly to the welcoming word, we add a blank character to the welcome note. This is followed by the name and a concluding exclamation mark. You see: it is no problem to add several strings in succession, and you can add both string variables as well as string constants.

4 Output the concatenated result string.

```
// concatenation of strings
import java.lang.*;

public class StringDemo2
  {
 public static void main(String[] args)
     {
     String welcoming_word  = "Hello";
     String name    = "Paul Watkinson";
     String output;
```

```
      output = welcoming_word + " " + name + "!";
      System.out.println(output);
   }
}
```

5 Save, compile and execute the program (Figure 6.6).

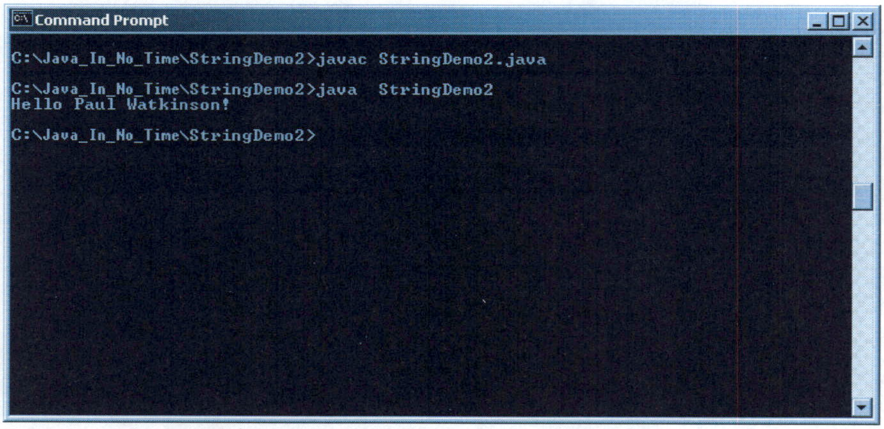

Figure 6.6: Output of the concatenated string.

Special characters in strings

The string `"Paul Watkinson"` contains only one set of quotation marks. Single quotation marks do not represent any problem in strings, but what can happen if we have to draft a string that contains double quotation marks:

`"Paul said "Hello!""`

It is clear that this cannot work. If the compiler comes across the double quotation marks when converting the source code, it knows that a string follows. Then it goes on reading character by character until it finds another double quotation mark that signals the end of the string. The string therefore reads `"Sean said"`. After that there is an identifier `Hello!` that is not defined anywhere and another string `""` that does not fit into this place. The compiler is confused. It surrenders and outputs a series of error messages.

To eliminate the error, we have to show the computer that the double quotation marks around `Hello!` are not the string-end characters but normal characters that belong to the text of the string. Therefore we put so-called escape characters \ in front of the quotation marks:

`"Paul said \"Hello!\"";`

Sequence	Task
\a	Beep
\n	New line
\t	Horizontal tabulator
\\	Backslash
\"	Double quotation marks

Table 6.3: The fundamental Escape sequences.

Manipulating strings

Stringing together and the output of strings are tasks that frequently arise in programming, but of course they are not the only ones. In this section we will see how strings can be compared with each other, how to determine their length, and how to look for characters in strings. In the next chapter you will also learn how to convert numbers into strings (and the other way round).

Determining the length of a string

The `String` class has a special method called `length()`. It returns the number to the single characters. This is sometimes very useful. Let's take a look at its use:

```
String str = "Hello Paul, how are you?";
int length = str.length();
```

Searching a string within another string

A typical operation on strings is the search for partial strings. For this purpose, there is the method `indexOf()` in `String`:

```
string str = "Hello Paul, how are you?";
```

```
string search pattern = "are";

int pos = str.indexOf(search pattern);
```

This method returns the position of the first appearance of the search pattern in the `String` object, whose `indexOf` method has been called. The individual characters of a string are numbered from zero onwards. If we therefore were to search for `Hello` in the above example, the result of the index would be 0, since the first character of `Hello` is in the 0 position. If the search pattern is not available, the value –1 is returned.

Replacing particular characters in a character string

Sometimes we have to replace all occurrences of a specific character in an existing string. The `String` class provides the method `replace()` for this purpose:

```
string str = "XXXXXX ----- XXXXX";

str = str.replace('-', 'X');
```

Here, we replace all – characters with X. `replace()`, returning a new `String` object as a return value, which is assigned `str` again.

Now, let's practice using the strings a little.

1 Begin a program and draft the following program framework.

```
// Three Chinese people
import java.lang.*;

public class Three_Chinese_people{
  public static void main(String[] args)
     {
     }
  }
```

2 Create a string variable that is initialised with the text `"Three Chinese people with a double-bass"`.

```
// Three Chinese people
import java.lang.*;

public class Three_Chinese_people
  {
  public static void main(String[] args)
     {
     String text = "Three Chinese people with a double bass";
     }
  }
```

3 Using the `replace()` method, make sure that all vocals become i. Output the result.

```
// Three Chinese people
import java.lang.*;

public class Three_Chinese_people
   {
   public static void main(String[] args)
      {
      String text  = "Three Chinese people with a double
bass";

      text = text.replace('e','i');
      text = text.replace('a','i');
      text = text.replace('o','i');

      System.out.println();    // give blank line
      System.out.println(text);
      }
   }
```

4 Save and compile the program. Then execute it (Figure 6.7).

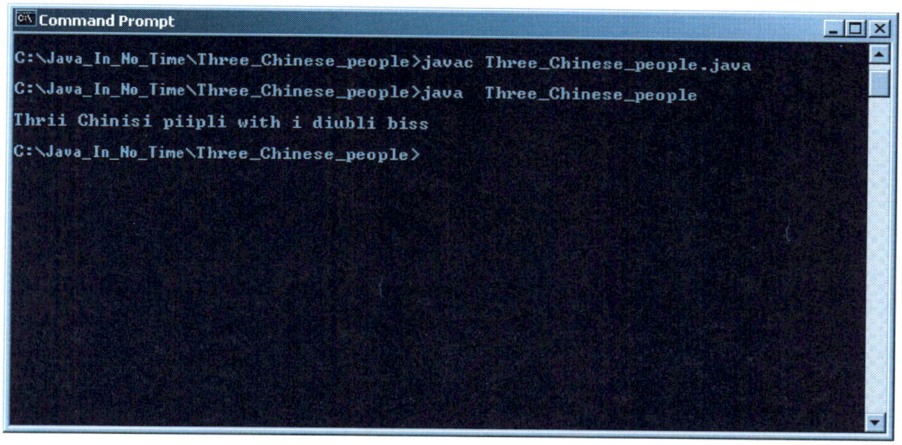

```
Command Prompt
C:\Java_In_No_Time\Three_Chinese_people>javac Three_Chinese_people.java

C:\Java_In_No_Time\Three_Chinese_people>java  Three_Chinese_people

Thrii Chinisi piipli with i diubli biss

C:\Java_In_No_Time\Three_Chinese_people>
```

Figure 6.7: Output of the modified string.

Recess: memory management for strings

If you have read about memory occupancy for elementary data types in Chapter 5, you may be wondering what the memory occupancy for strings looks like.

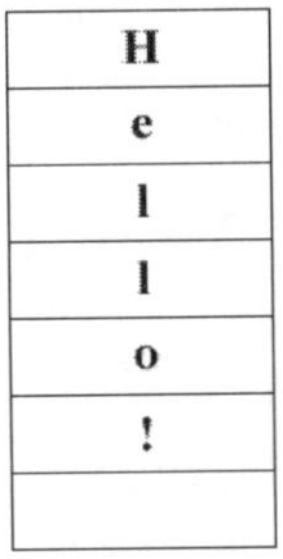

H
e
l
l
o
!

Figure 6.8: A string in the working memory (each character takes up 16 bits = 2 bytes).

Strings are simply stored character by character one after the other in the memory (Figure 6.8). For the compiler to be able to know where the string ends, it saves further information in the class.

Things become more problematic if you save a string such as "Hello" in a `String` variable and then assigns a string "Welcome" to a variable or adds a string "Paul".

```
String str = "Hello";
str = "Welcome";
```

or

```
str += "Paul";
```

Here, the problem is that the string that will be saved in the variable is extended. But, at this point, we know from Chapter 5 that it is not possible to extend the memory after it has been reserved for a particular variable. However, you have seen that it is possible to assign new strings to `String` variables, to add or insert other strings to, and remove sub strings. How is this possible?

The solution is hidden in the implementation of the class `String`. If, for example, you assign a new string to a `String` variable, the class reserves a completely new memory area for the string. The old memory area is opened and the `String` variable with the new memory area is added to it.

To conclude, we can establish that the class `String` not only provides a series of powerful methods for processing strings, but also spares us from some annoying tasks such as memory management.

Chapter 7

Reading and outputting data

Most programs are designed to exchange data with other users, i.e. they accept the data to be processed via the keyboard and output the result on the console. In this chapter we will see how this process works.

Outputting data on the console

In Chapter 4, we learned that you output data on the console and display it on the screen by using the method `System.out.println()`.

This method is very practical. You can distribute constants and variables in various combinations:

- individual string/number constants:

```
System.out.println("Hello World");

System.out.println(245);
```

- individual string/number variables:

```
int var = 245;

String text = "Hello World";

System.out.println(text);

System.out.println(var);
```

- any combination of variables and constants; individual components are interlinked by the + operator:

```
System.out.println("Hello World" + "number = "+ var);
```

As well as `println()`, there is the almost identical method `print()`. The only difference is that no line break is inserted at the end. Therefore, there can be several outputs in the same line.

Reading data from the console

Unfortunately, the reverse of this, i.e. reading numbers and characters that need to be processed by the program, is a bit more specific. For this, you need some special classes and mechanisms from the package `java.io`, which you should now get used to using. These will be discussed during the course of the book.

The use of data sent to the Java program from the keyboard is carried out in two steps:

1. To begin with, the Java runtime environment must establish a connection with the keyboard.

2. The characters typed in by the user need to be converted into suitable data types.

Reading input from the keyboard

```
BufferedReader keyboard = new
          BufferedReader(new
InputStreamReader(System.in));
```

This looks really hideous! But don't be deterred; just accept these lines as they are, because you will understand what this means later on. Here, it is enough to know that there are just three classes involved (`BufferedReader`, `InputStreamReader` and `System.in`), which somehow work together and return the variable `keyboard`. This establishes the connection to the keyboard.

Since `keyboard` is of the class type `BufferedReader`, the special method `readLine()` is available that, together with the input from the user, is provided as a string:

```
string input;
```

```
input = keyboard.readLine();
```

Now we have almost finished. If the user wants to enter a string (e.g. a name) we are now ready and can use the string variable `input` if necessary. But what if the user has actually entered a number? Then we have to convert it into the correct data type.

Converting strings into numbers

The conversion of a number that exists as a string into a "real" number is carried out using special methods that are available for any elementary data type:

```
int integernumber = integer.parseint(input);
```

```
float floatnumber = float.parsefloat(input);
```

```
double doublenumber = double.parsedouble(input);
```

The prerequisite for the use of these methods is, of course, that the string that is to be submitted has to contain something meaningful. The compiler, with the best will in the world, could not generate a number from the character string `"Hello"`!

Now it's time for us to try and put what we have learnt into practice. As an example, we will use the program `Fahrenheit.java` from Chapter 6.

1 Create a new program, `Fahrenheit2.java`, and type in or copy the source text of `Fahrenheit.java`. Remember to adapt the class name.

```java
// Fahrenheit conversion with keyboard entries
import java.lang.*;

public class Fahrenheit2
    {
    public static void main(String[] args)
        {
        double fahrenheit;
        double centigrade;

        fahrenheit = 20;
        centigrade = (fahrenheit - 32) * 5.0 / 9.0;

        System.out.println(fahrenheit +
                            "correspond to degree Fahrenheit
");
        System.out.println(centigrade + "degree
centigrade");
        }
    }
```

Using this program, you can convert a temperature entry from degrees Fahrenheit into degrees centigrade. However, the program is impractical in this respect because you also have to

- load the source text;

- assign another value to the variable `fahrenheit`;

- compile the program again and execute it

for each Fahrenheit value that you need to calculate. You cannot give such a program to your friends to use, as it will not work in practice without a Java compiler (apart from always converting 20 degrees Fahrenheit into degrees centigrade).

However, if we refine the program so that the Fahrenheit value is queried by the user, we get a meaningful program with which you can convert any Fahrenheit value into centigrade.

2 Install an input that asks the user to input the Fahrenheit value.

```
// fahrenheit conversion with keyboard entry
import java.lang.*;

public class Fahrenheit2
    {
    public static void main(string[] args)
        {
        double fahrenheit;
        double centigrade;

      system.out.print("Temperature in fahrenheit: ");

        centigrade = (fahrenheit - 32) * 5.0 / 9.0;

        system.out.println(fahrenheit +
                        "degrees fahrenheit correspond to
");
        system.out.println(centigrade + "degrees
centigrade");

        }
  }
```

3 Create a variable that is connected to the keyboard.

```
// fahrenheit conversion with keyboard entry
import java.lang.*;
import java.io.*;

public class Fahrenheit2
    {
    public static void main(string[] args)
                                    throws IOException
        {
        double fahrenheit;
        double centigrade;

        System.out.print("Temperature in fahrenheit: ");

        // Connection with the keyboard
        BufferedReader keyboard =
                new BufferedReader(
                new InputStreamReader(System.in));

        centigrade = (fahrenheit - 32) * 5.0 / 9.0;

        System.out.println(fahrenheit +
                        "degree fahrenheit correspond to");
        System.out.println(centigrade + "degrees
centigrade");

        }
  }
```

In this step, we need to take three things into account. First of all, the classes (`BufferedReader` etc.) from the `java.io` package are required, therefore the corresponding `import` statement must be inserted at the beginning of the program.

Next, insert the line for the `keyboard` variable. We have already explained this process above. In doing so, you create the connection with the keyboard.

Finally, `throws 10Exception` also has to be added after the name of the method `main()`. Unfortunately, we cannot go into more detail of this in this book. This is additional information for the compiler, so that it knows that the following source text contains special statements that can go wrong during the execution (in our example, if the connection to the keyboard on `BufferedReader`take is not achieved).

4 Read a line from the keyboard as a string.

```
// Fahrenheit conversion with keyboard entry
import java.lang.*;
import java.io.*;

public class Fahrenheit2
    {
    public static void main(string[] args)
                                        throws IOException
        {
        double fahrenheit;
        double centigrade;

        System.out.print("temperature in fahrenheit: ");

        // connection with the keyboard
        BufferedReader keyboard =
                        new BufferedReader(
                        new InputStreamReader(System.in));

        String input = keyboard.readLine();

        centigrade = (fahrenheit - 32) * 5.0 / 9.0;

        System.out.println(fahrenheit +
                            "degrees fahrenheit correspond
to");
        System.out.println(centigrade + "degrees
Centigrade");

        }
    }
```

5 Convert the input string read from the keyboard into a `double` number.

```
// Fahrenheit conversion with keyboard entry
import java.lang.*;
import java.io.*;

public class Fahrenheit2
    {
    public static void main(String[] args)
                                    throws IOException
        {
        double fahrenheit;
        double centigrade;

        System.out.print("temperature in fahrenheit: ");

        // connection with the keyboard
        BufferedReader keyboard =
                        new BufferedReader(
                        new InputStreamReader(System.in));

        String input = keyboard.readLine();
        fahrenheit = Double.parseDouble(input);

        centigrade = (fahrenheit - 32) * 5.0 / 9.0;

        System.out.println(fahrenheit +
                            "degrees fahrenheit correspond
to");
        System.out.println(centigrade + "degrees
centigrade");

        }
  }
```

6 Save the program as `Fahrenheit2.java`, compile and execute it.

If you execute the program, at the beginning the statement:

```
temperature in fahrenheit:
```

appears on the console.

After that the program seems to stop. But not at the output with `System.out.print()` but at the line

```
string input = keyboard.readLine();
```

This expects the user to type in a value and send it to the program by clicking on the ⏎ button. In doing so, the character string is saved in the variable `input` and the program can be continued (Figure 7.1).

```
Command Prompt                                              _ □ ×

C:\Java_In_No_Time\Fahrenheit2>javac Fahrenheit2.java

C:\Java_In_No_Time\Fahrenheit2>java Fahrenheit2
temperature in fahrenheit: 84
84.0 degrees fahrenheit correspond to
28.88888888888889 degrees centigrade

C:\Java_In_No_Time\Fahrenheit2>_
```

Figure 7.1: Output of the Fahrenheit2 *program.*

Limiting decimal places

If you look at the output of the Fahrenheit program, the unnecessarily high number of displayed fractional digits is a bit annoying. If you want to know how warm 84 degrees Fahrenheit is, it is enough to know that it is about 28.9 degrees centigrade. An output that is correct to ten fractional digits is more disruptive than useful.

Java offers no direct support, but because we already know something about the data types, we can help ourselves.

The trick is to juggle with the data types `int` and `double`. The result shows almost endless fractional digits. But let's assume that we just want to have two positions after the point.

You can achieve this by multiplying the original `double` result by 100 (= two decimal places) and then pressing the new value into a variable of the `int` type (we call this a cast). Because of this, the compiler rejects the other fractional digits and we only have to reverse the multiplication with a division and file this in a `double` variable.

Adaptation of the Fahrenheit program

Let's adapt the output of the Fahrenheit program so that the degree values are always given with only two fractional digits.

1 Begin a new program, `Fahrenheit3.java`, and type in or copy the code from `Fahrenheit2.java`. Remember to adapt the class names.

```
// fahrenheit conversion with
// keyboard entry and 2 fractional digits
import java.lang.*;
import java.io.*;

public class Fahrenheit3
    {
    public static void main(String[] args)
                                    throws IOException
        {
        double fahrenheit;
        double centigrade;

        System.out.print("temperature in fahrenheit: ");

        // connection with the keyboard
        BufferedReader keyboard = new BufferedReader(
                    new InputStreamReader(System.in));

        String input = keyboard.readLine();
        fahrenheit = Double.parseDouble(input);

        centigrade = (fahrenheit - 32) * 5.0 / 9.0;

        System.out.println(fahrenheit +
                        " degrees fahrenheit correspond
to");
        System.out.println(centigrade + " degrees
centigrade");

        }
    }
```

2 Now add a statement that multiplies the calculated centigrade value by 100 and casts it in an `int` variable.

```java
// Fahrenheit conversion with
// keyboard entry and 2 fractional digits
import java.lang.*;
import java.io.*;

public class Fahrenheit3
    {
    public static void main(String[] args)
                                        throws IOException
        {
        double fahrenheit;
        double centigrade;

        System.out.print("Temperature in Fahrenheit: ");

        // Connection with the keyboard
        BufferedReader keyboard = new BufferedReader(
                    new InputStreamReader(System.in));

        String input = keyboard.readLine();
        fahrenheit = Double.parseDouble(input);

        centigrade = (fahrenheit - 32) * 5.0 / 9.0;
        int temp = (int) (centigrade * 100.0);

        System.out.println(fahrenheit +
                        " degrees Fahrenheit correspond
to");
        System.out.println(centigrade + " degrees
centigrade");

        }
    }
```

We have to force the compiler into an `int` variable using the statement `(int)` before the actual expression. Also notice the bracketing of `(centigrade * 100.0)`. This is necessary so that the result of the multiplication (i.e. the whole bracket) is cast, and not the value of centigrade.[1]

---

1. (int) centigrade * 100 would mean that first the value is cast in centigrade and then the multiplication by 100 is carried out; then the fractional digits disappear.

3 Now reverse the multiplication again.

```
// Fahrenheit conversion with
// keyboard entry and 2 fractional digits
import java.lang.*;
import java.io.*;

public class Fahrenheit3
    {
    public static void main(String[] args)
                                    throws IOException
        {
        double fahrenheit;
        double centigrade;

        System.out.print("temperature in fahrenheit: ");

        // connection with the keyboard
        BufferedReader keyboard = new BufferedReader(
                        new InputStreamReader(System.in));

        String input = keyboard.readLine();
        fahrenheit = Double.parseDouble(input);

        centigrade = (fahrenheit - 32) * 5.0 / 9.0;
        int temp = (int) (centigrade * 100.0);
        centigrade = temp / 100.0;
        System.out.println(fahrenheit +
                        " degrees fahrenheit correspond
to ");
        System.out.println(centigrade + " degrees
centigrade");
        }
    }
```

4 Save the program as Fahrenheit3.java, compile and execute it (Figure 7.2).

Figure 7.2: Output with only two decimal places.

101

Chapter 8

Comparing and branching

In principle, programs are executed sequentially, i.e. statement by statement. With the help of keywords that are specially anchored in the programming language, the programmer can break up and allow statements or blocks of statements to be executed several times one after the other (for/while), under certain conditions (if), or alternatively (if-else/switch). In this chapter you will learn how to compare values and execute different statements according to the result of this comparison. (We will look at the multiple execution of statements in the next chapter).

Comparing numbers and strings

Up until now, you have learnt how to set up variables for numbers or strings, how to assign variables to these variables, and how to count with numbers or manipulate strings. However, we have left out an important topic: how can we compare numbers (or strings)?

Comparisons are relatively useless if there is no option of reacting to the results of the comparison. However, we were lacking the tools to do this until now. We will discuss this in the next section and we will now show how to compare numbers and strings.

Let's assume that you have defined the following variables at the start of a program:

```
int i = 3;
int j = 50;
```

Below, you want to test in the code whether the variable i always contains the value 3. The operator == serves this purpose:

```
i == 3
```

> **CAUTION**
>
> *Do not forget that = is the assignment operator and == is the equality operator. If you want to test whether the variable i is equal to 3 but write* i = 3 *by mistake, the compiler will take issue with this.*

The == operator checks whether the two operands (here the variable i and the constant value 3) have an equal value.

Return values of comparisons

If you add two numbers, for example

```
i + j
```

it is clear that this operation returns the sum of the added values as a result:

```
int result;

result = i + j;      // now the result has the value 53
```

The question now is which values return the comparison i == 3?

In Java comparisons are always interpreted as questions that can be answered with either yes or no. The comparison i == 3 therefore represents the question, "Is the value of i equal to 3?" The answer is either yes or no. Java codes these values using two special keywords: `true` and `false`.

Java also has its own data type called `pool`, whose variables can only be assigned the boolean logic values `true` and `false`. We could also write:

```
int i = 3;
int j = 50;

boolean result;
result = false;          // the result is now false
result = i == 3;         // the result now is true
```

Operators for comparisons

You have now seen how, using the `==` operator (which should not be confused with the `=` operator), you can check whether values of the two operands are equal. But Java also knows a number of other operators with which you can carry out various comparisons (in Table 8.1 it could be i = 3 and j = 50):

Operator	Meaning	Example
==	Equal	`i == 4` // false
!=	Unequal	`i! = 4` // true
<	Less than	`i < j` // true
>	Greater than	`i > j` // false
<=	Less than or equal to	`i <= 5` // true
>=	Greater than or equal to	`i >= 3` // true

Table 8.1: Comparison operators for numbers.

Comparing strings

As with the simple arithmetic operators, strings take on a special position. Unfortunately, silly errors can be installed in the program since the `==`-operator is also feasible with strings and, in certain cases, it even gives correct comparison results.

Test on equality

For the test on the equality of two strings, the method `equals()` is used which possesses every variable of the `String` type. `equals()` returns a boolean truth value, therefore `true` or `false` as a result:

Let's consider the following `String` variables:

```
String name1 = "Dave";
String name2 = "Peter";
```

The comparison then looks like the following:

```
boolean result;

result = name1.equals(name2);
```

Lexicographical comparisons

In addition to this direct comparison, character strings can also be compared with each other relatively, i.e. you can compare them from a lexicographical point of view. What does this mean? "Dave" is lexicographically smaller than "Peter" because, in the alphabet, D comes before P. In the same way, we can say that "Peter" is lexicographically larger than "Dave". If the first letters were identical, the result would depend on the second letter, etc. You will become familiar with this. Phone books, for example, are ordered lexicographically.

NOTE

Actually, a computer does not compare characters. It requires numbers and internally converts all characters (from strings) into ASCII code. This code assigns a specific number to each character. However, since in the ASCII code characters are to be found in the same order as they appear in the alphabet, this represents a normal alphabetical comparison for normal words (without special characters such as ! or #).

Furthermore, it must be taken into account that:

- In string comparisons, upper-case letters are always smaller than lower-case letters (Z is therefore smaller than a), because the upper-case letters in the ASCII code stand in front of the lower-case letters and therefore have lower number values;

- as a last criterion, there is also the string length ("game" is therefore smaller than "games" or "gameplan").

Each `String` variable possesses the method `compareTo()` for lexicographical comparisons. For two strings, a and b, it returns the following values:

- a negative value, if a is lexicographically less than b;

- zero, if a = b;

- a positive value, if a > b.

Here are a few examples:

```
String name = "Jonathan";
int result;

result = name.compareTo("Dave");          // result < 0
result = name.compareTo("Peter");         // result > 0
result = name.compareTo("Christopher");       // result < 0

result = name.compareTo("Jonathan");      // result = 0
```

CAUTION

When using `compareTo()`, *you will frequently notice that only specific number values are returned as results, e.g. –1. However, you cannot rely on them. Therefore, do not write any program that runs on the assumption that if* `compareTo()` *returns the value –1 it is then "less".*

Yes or no? – The if branching

Occasionally, there is the problem that you want to execute a statement or a block of statements only if certain prerequisites are fulfilled. So, for example, a program that calculates the square root of a number that has been entered should guarantee that the number that is entered is a positive number, since the square root of a negative number is not defined. This is possible with the `if` condition.

General syntax

The common syntax of the `if` condition looks like this:

```
if (condition)
    {
    statement (s);
    }
```

This construction can also be read like a conditional sentence:

"If the condition is filled, then (and only then) the statements are executed."

During the execution of the program, the condition is evaluated first. The condition is nothing more than a comparison. If the result of the comparison is returned as `true`, the condition is fulfilled and the instructions block belonging to the `if` condition is executed; otherwise, the program continues with the next statement after the statement block.

A single statement or a block of statements can follow the `if` condition. A statement must always have a semicolon at the end of it. If a block of statements is to be executed (i.e. several statements), this will need to be put in curly brackets.

Conditional execution of statements

In Chapter 6, you learnt about the mathematical function `sqrt()`, with which the square root of a number can be calculated. As you know, the square root function is only defined for positive numbers. We now want to write a program that allows the user to enter a number and calculates the square root from this. Since we cannot be sure that the user will not enter a value smaller than zero, we check the entry in the program with the help of an if condition.

> **NOTE**
>
> *Checking for correctness is a typical area of use for the `if` condition.*

1 Begin a new program, `Root.java`, and start creating the following basic framework.

```java
// root calculation
import java.lang.*;

public class Root
    {
    public static void main(String[] args)
                                throws IOException
        {
        String input;
        double value root;

        }
    }
```

2 Read a number entered from the keyboard.

```java
// root calculation
import java.lang.*;
import java.io.*;

public class Root
    {
    public static void main(String[] args)
                                throws IOException
        {
        String input;
        double value, root;
        BufferedReader keyboard;

        System.out.println();
        System.out.println("Program for the calculation of the
root ");
        System.out.print("enter a number, please: ");

        // Keyboard input
        keyboard = new BufferedReader(
                new InputStreamReader(System.in));
        input = keyboard.readLine();
        value= Double.parseDouble(input);
        }
    }
```

You should already be familiar with the reading of data that have been entered via the keyboard. We create a variable of the class type `BufferedReader`, which, as shown, is connected with the input current of the keyboard. The user's input is read using the method `readLine()` and saved in a variable of the `double` type by means of `Double.parse Double()`. Do not forget the necessary `import` statement for the `java.io` package, as well as the offset `throws IOException` after `main()`. If necessary, read Chapter 7 again.

Check, using the `if` condition, whether the user has input a positive number. If so, the root is calculated.

```
// root calculation
import java.lang.*;
import java.io.*;

public class Root
    {
    public static void main(String[] args)
                                throws IOException
        {
        String input;
        double value, root;
        BufferedReader keyboard;

        System.out.println();
        System.out.println("program for the calculation of the
root");
        System.out.print("feed a number, please: ");

        // keyboard input
        keyboard = new BufferedReader(new
                            InputStreamReader(System.in));
        input = keyboard.readLine();
        value = Double.parseDouble(input);

        if (value>= 0)
          {
          root = Math.sqrt(value);
          system.out.println("root out "+ value +
                            " is "+ root);
        }

        system.out.println("program is finished");
        }
    }
```

The `if` conditions begin with the keyword `if`. The condition that has to be checked follows in brackets. In our example, the condition is that the value in the variable `value` has to be greater than or equal to zero.

if (value >= 0)

The statement block comes directly below the `if` condition, which is controlled by the `if` condition. In our example, this means that the `sqrt` function and the output of the result are only executed if the `if` condition is met (therefore, if the value in `value` greater than or equal to 0).

```
if (value >= 0)
    {
    root = Math.sqrt(value);
    system.out.println("root out "+ value +
                        " is "+ root);
    }
```

> **TIP**
>
> *Because the statement block is indented a little, by looking at the
> source text you can see that the block belongs to the if condition.*

Under the statement block of the if condition, we provide a short note
stating that the program is now ended. Since this statement is no longer
controlled by the if condition, it is always executed (make sure that this is
the case by also entering negative numbers when testing).

> **CAUTION**
>
> *Never place a semicolon after the condition. The compiler would
> interpret this as an empty statement. An if condition that is true
> would only refer to this blank statement, which means that nothing
> more would be done to this statement, and the following statement
> block would always be processed.*

3 Save the program as Root.java, compile and execute it (Figure 8.1).

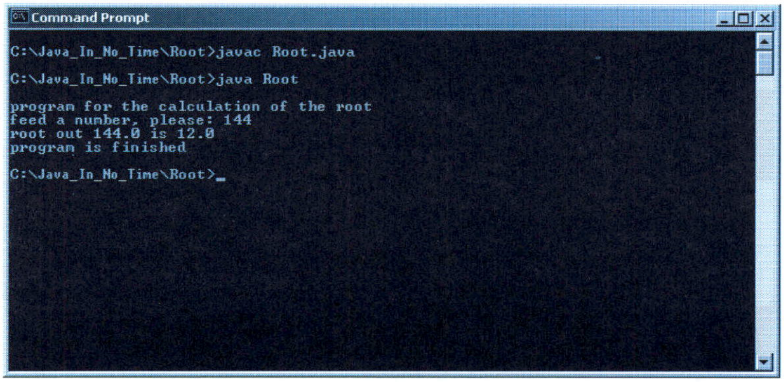

Figure 8.1: Output of the root program.

The else alternative

By using an `if-else` construction you can execute one block or another depending on a condition. We want to make use of this in our root program to point out errors to the user in case of a negative input.

1 The starting point is the program from the last section.

2 Add the `if` condition to the statement block of the else block.

```java
// root calculation
import java.lang.*;
import java.io.*;

public class Root
    {
    public static void main(String[] args)
                                    throws IOException
      {
      String input;
      double value, root;
      BufferedReader keyboard;

      System.out.println();
      System.out.println("program for the calculation of the
root");
      System.out.print("feed a number, please: ");

      // keyboard input
      keyboard = new BufferedReader(new
                            InputStreamReader(System.in));
      input = keyboard.readLine();
      value = Double.parseDouble(input);

      if (value >= 0)
         {
         root = Math.sqrt(value);
         System.out.println("root out" + value +
                         " is "+ root);
        }
      else
         {
         System.out.println(
            "Root of negative number not possible");
        }

     System.out.println("program is finished");
     }
  }
```

This program reads a number from the keyboard and outputs its root if a number that has been input is greater than or equal to zero. If a negative number is input, the statement block is ignored due to the `if` condition, and instead the `else` block is executed.

3 Compile the program and execute it (Figure 8.2).

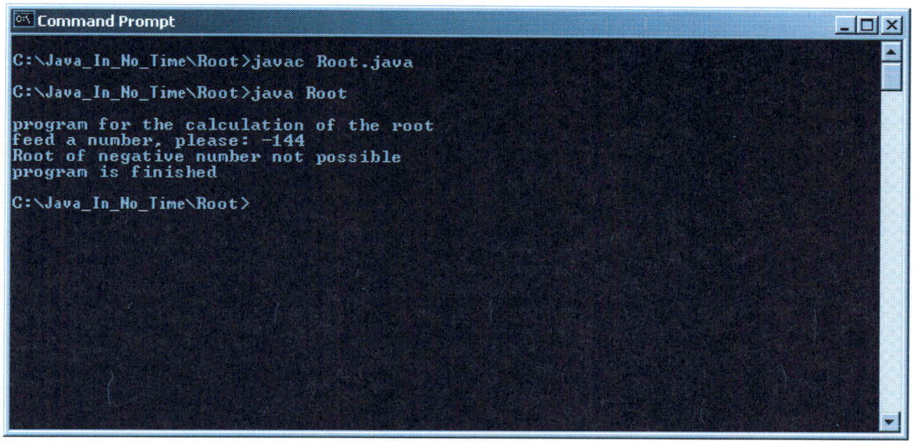

Figure 8.2: Output of the program for negative input.

Nesting if-else branches

Sometimes we want to distinguish more than two cases. Then it can be advisable to nest several `if-else` conditions.

Let's assume that you want to write a quiz program that is targeted according to the age of the participants of the quiz and therefore requires a selection of questions. Branch as follows:

```java
if (age < 20) {
   System.out.println("Who is Britney Spears?");
   }
   else if (age < 50) {
      System.out.println("Who is George Michael?");
      }
      else {
         System.out.println("Who is George Formby?");
         }
```

This construction is evaluated as follows:

- If the participant is under 20, The question is: "Who is Britney Spears?"
- If the participant is between 20 and 50, the question is: "Who is George Michael?"
- If the participant is 50 or older, the question is: "Who is George Formby?"

The switch branch

If you want to repeatedly split up the execution of the program depending on the value of a variable, you can use the `switch` construction.

Common syntax

```
switch(expression)
{
    case constant1: Statements;
                        break;
    case constant2: Statements;;
                        break;
    case constant3: Statements;;
                        break;
    case constant4: Statements;;
                        break;
    default:  Statements;;
}
```

An integer variable or a character (Typ `char`) can be given as an expression. During the execution of the program, the value of this variable is then compared with the `case` constants that are within the `switch` statement. If the value of the variable agrees with a `case` constant, the accompanying statements are executed. The final `break` statement makes sure that the program is continued after this with the next statement under the `switch` branch.

Three points are to be followed:

- Give integer constants as simply numbers (`3`, `423`), character constants stand in single quotation marks (`'a'`, `'D'`).

- If you do not complete statements to a `case` block with `break`, then the statements of the underlying `case` block will also be executed. You can do this consciously, but you can also cause faults in this way.

- The statement block belonging to `default` is branched if the check of the `switch` expression produces no agreement with the `case` mark.

We will illustrate the use of the `switch` branch with an example: the construction of the console menu.

How do I equip my statements with a menu?

If you eventually write more complex programs, these programs will, in all probability, be created in such a way that the program is able to carry out not only one task (as in the case of our root program), but several connected tasks. For example, a program for calculating vectors could be created in such a way that one can read into a vector with the program and then carry out different operations on this vector (addition or subtraction of a second vector, calculation of length, calculation of the scalar or vector products, etc.).

In such a case, you need to enable the user to choose what the program shall do next. One option, for example, would be the output of a menu.

1 Create a new program, `vector.java`, and begin with the usual basic framework.

```
// vector calculations
import java.lang.*;
import java.io.*;

public class vector
    {
    public static void main(String[] args)
                                    throws IOException
        {
        }
    }
```

2 Output the menu as series of options and read the user's input.

```java
// vector calculations
import java.lang.*;
import java.io.*;

public class vector
    {
    public static void main(String[] args)
                                    throws   IOException

        {

        System.out.println();
        System.out.println("enter vectors    <1>");
        System.out.println("add up vectors   <2>");
        System.out.println("add up vectors   <3>");
        System.out.println("add up vectors   <4>");
        System.out.println("add up vectors   <5>");
        System.out.println("add up vectors   <6>");
        System.out.println("finish program   <0>");

        System.out.println("your selection: ");

        BufferedReader t = new BufferedReader(
                    new InputStream(System.in));

        String input = t.readLine();
        int selection = Integer.parseInt(input);
        }
    }
```

Because the user cannot choose the commands of the menu with a click of the mouse, as in the menu list of a Windows application, we give each command a code number, which the user must type on the keyboard in order to have the corresponding menu command executed.

After the output of the menu, we ask the user to input the code number of one of the menu options that are offered, read the input with readLine() and create an integral value using Integer.parseInt().

3 Introduce the `switch` branch.

CAUTION

In the switch statement only `int`, `long` *and* `char` *variables can be used.*

```java
// vector calculations
import java.lang.*;
import java.io.*;

public class vector
   {
   public static void main(String[] args)
                                 throws IOException
      {
      System.out.println();
      System.out.println("enter vectors          <1>");
      System.out.println("add up vectors         <2>");
      System.out.println("subtract vectors       <3>");
      System.out.println("scalar product         <4>");
      System.out.println("vector product         <5>");
      System.out.println("vector length          <6>");
      System.out.println("finish program         <0>");

      System.out.print("your selection: ");

      BufferedReader t = new BufferedReader(
                  new InputStreamReader(System.in));

      String input = t.readLine();
      int selection = Integer.parseInt(input);

      // react to selection
      switch(selection)
        {
        }

      }
   }
```

4 Draft the different alternatives in the `switch` statement.

```java
// vector calculations
import java.lang.*;
import java.io.*;

public class vector
    {
    public static void main(String[] args)
                                throws IOException
        {
        System.out.println();
        System.out.println("enter vectors      <1>");
        System.out.println("add up vectors     <2>");
        System.out.println("subtract vectors   <3>");
        System.out.println("scalar product     <4>");
        System.out.println("vector product     <5>");
        System.out.println("vector length      <6>");
        System.out.println("finish program     <0>");

        System.out.print("your selection: ");

        BufferedReader t = new BufferedReader(
                        new InputStreamReader(System.in));

        String input = t.readLine();
        int selection = Integer.parseInt(input);

        // react to selection
        switch(selection)
            {
            case 0: System.out.println("finish program");
                    break;
            case 1: System.out.println("enter vector");
                    break;
            case 2: System.out.println("add up vectors");
                    break;
            case 3: System.out.println("subtract vectors");
                    break;
            case 4: System.out.println("scalar product");
                    break;
            case 5: System.out.println("vector product");
                    break;
            case 6: System.out.println("length of the vector");
                    break;
            default:System.out.println("false input!");
                    break;
            }
        }
    }
```

The single branches of the `switch statement` always begin with the keyword `case`, followed by a constant (e.g. 1, 6 or 'a', 'b' for char variables). During the execution of the program, it is checked whether one of the `case` constants agrees with the actual value of the `switch` variable (`selection, in the example`). If so, the program execution jumps to the code next to the `case` mark.

Each `case` block is closed with a `break` statement. The `break` statement makes sure that the whole `switch` statement is exited and the program is continued with the next statement under the `switch` statement.

When there is a `default` block (you can also leave it out), the program execution jumps to this block if the actual value of the `switch` variable (in the `selection` example) does not agree with any of the `case` constants. If you set the `default` block at the end of the `switch` statement, you do not have to close it with a `break` statement, though this is not without some use.

5 Save the program as `vector.java`, compile and execute it (Figure 8.3).

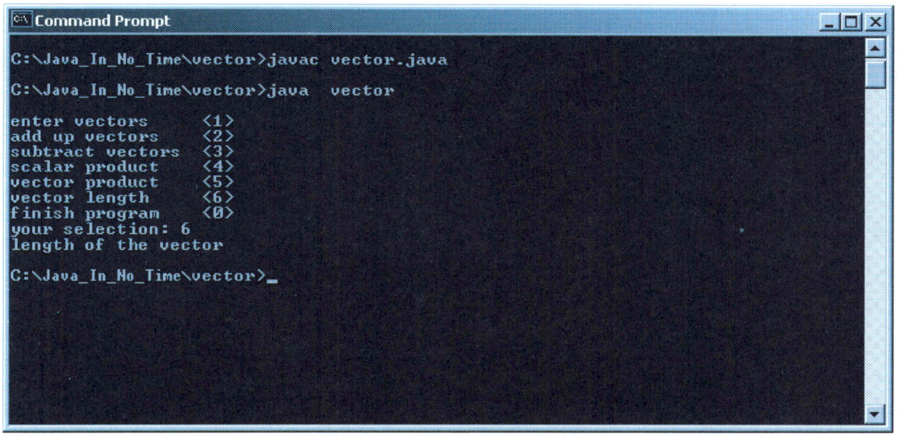

Figure 8.3: Output of the menu.

NOTE

We will expand and perfect the vector program and the menu later. In Chapter 12, we will introduce a version of a program that is implemented using classes and methods.

119

Chapter 9

Multiple execution
of statements

In the previous chapter you saw how two statement blocks could be executed alternatively. In this chapter, we learn how to execute an instruction block several times in a row through the use of loops.

What are loops used for?

Loops are used to execute a statement block several times in a row.

You may ask what the point is of a row of statements being executed after each other several times. Indeed, there may only be a few programs in which there is the need to be able to execute the same action over and over.

Now, of course, it makes no sense to assign the same value to a variable *x* times, or write the same output *x* times in succession on the screen:

```
int square = 9;
System.out.println(square);
System.out.println(square);
```

However, notice that the content of the variables can also change in successive identical statements:

```
int loop = 0;
++loop;   // loop = 1
++loop;   // loop = 2
++loop;   // loop = 3
...
```

You can see already that if the correct statements are combined, then the multiple execution of a sequence of statements can be quite interesting. Therefore, the following statement sequence outputs the square of the number 1:

```
int loop = 0;
++loop;
System.out.println(loop * loop);
```

If you add further copies of the last two statements to these lines, you output the squares of the first individual numbers one after the other:

```
int loop = 0;
++loop;
System.out.println(loop * loop); // output: 1

 ++loop;
System.out.println(loop * loop); // output: 4

++loop;
System.out.println(loop * loop); // output: 9

++loop;
System.out.println(loop * loop); // output: 16
```

Repeating the instructions directly is unsightly, time consuming, and prone to errors. It would be easier and more and elegant to arrange the program so that it will execute statements in succession. You can do this with a loop.

The for loop

One of the two important loop variants is the `for` loop, which is used mostly if the programmer knows already from the start how often the loop is to be passed.

Common syntax

The common syntax of the `for` loop looks like this:

```
for (initialization; condition; alteration)
    {
    Statement(s);
    }
```

- `initialization`: Code that is executed at the first link to the loop. During the following loop passage, the statement is no longer needed and therefore it is not executed.

- `condition`: So long as the conditions are met, the statement block belonging to the `for` loop is executed; if this is not the case, then the loop is abandoned.

- `alteration`: The statement of this part of executed after every loop passage and before the recent check of the loop conditions.

How are loops controlled?

The three components `initialization`, `condition` and `alteration` all constitute the *loop header*. They contain code that determines how often the loops are executed (administered by the statement block that follows the loop head).

But how can you control how often a loop is executed?

Quite easily, with the help of a variable declared especially for this purpose, which serves as a type of counter for the run of the loop.

At the start, you put the loop variable on a start value (`Initialisation`). If the statement block of the loop is executed one or more times, you increase the loop variable (`reinitialisation`), until a particular value is exceeded, so that the loop condition is no longer met.

Let's look at the following code, for example:

```
int loop;

for(loop = 1; loop <= 5; ++loop)
   {
   // Statement
   }
```

The code begins with the declaration of the loop variable called `loop` here. During the joining of the loop, the loop variable must be assigned a start value. This happens in the statement: `loop = 1;` .

Then the condition is formulated, which determines how long the loop is executed: `loop <= 5;` . So long as the conditions are met, i.e. as long as the loop variable `loop` is less than or equal to 5, the loop is executed.

The third statement is executed after every statement block of the loop has been processed. This leads to the value of `loop` after five loop passages being greater than 5, with the consequence that the loop condition is no longer met and the loop is exited.

Execution of a loop

We will now show how the above loop is executed.

First of all, we will provide the loop with a genuine statement block so that our execution is not so abstract.

```
int loop;
int sum = 0;

for(loop = 1; loop <= 5; ++loop)
   {
   sum += loop;
   }

System.out.println("The sum of the first "+ (loop-1) +
             "Numbers are: " + sum);
```

> **CAUTION**
>
> *Note that the last statement in the loop header is not completed with a semicolon.*

During the joining of the loop, the loop variable `loop` is assigned the value 1.

Next, the loop condition is checked. Since it is met (the value of `loop` is less than 5), the statement block of the loop is executed. The variable `sum` is now added to the old value (0) of the value of `loop`.

After the execution of the statement block, the third statement of the loop header, ++loop, is executed. The loop variable `loop` therefore now contains the value 2.

Further execution of the loop always follows the same scheme:

1. The loop condition is checked.

2. If the condition is met, the statement block of the loop is executed.

3. After the processing of the statement block, the loop variable is incremented in the loop head in accordance with the third statement. Then we begin with step 1 again.

So `loop` takes on the values 1, 2, 3, 4 and 5 in succession, and in `sum` the values 1, 3, 6, 10 and 15 are saved in succession.

After the fifth passage of the loop, the increment statement is executed again. The variable `loop` then has the value 6. If the condition `loop <= 5` is now checked before joining the next loop passage, it shows the loop condition is no longer being met.

Consequently, since the statement block of the loop is no longer executed, the loop is abandoned, and the program is continued with the statement that follows the loop.

Calculating number sequences using loops

As an exercise, we will now implement a loop. With the help of this loop, the first 10 square numbers will be calculated and output.

1 Create a new program `ForLoop.java` and begin with the following basic framework:

```java
// square number using for loop
import java.lang.*;

public class ForLoop
    {
    public static void main(String[] args)
        {
        }
    }
```

2 Declare the loop variable and create the loop head with blank statement block.

```java
// square number using for loop
import java.lang.*;

public class ForLoop
    {
    public static void main(String[] args)
        {
        int loop;

        for(loop = 1; loop <= 10; ++loop)
            {
            }

        }
    }
```

> **CAUTION**
>
> *The last statements in the loop header cannot be closed with a semicolon. The same applies after the loop head, i.e. after the second round bracket.*

Because we want to calculate the first 10 square numbers, we initialise the loop variable with 1 and let it proceed in steps, up to and including 10 exponents. The condition is selected so that the loop is completed when the loop variable is greater than 10.

3 Draft the statement block of the loop.

```
// square number through for-loop
import java.lang.*;

public class ForLoop
    {
    public static void main(String[] args)
        {
        int loop;
        int square;
        for(loop = 1; loop <= 10; ++loop)
            {
            square = loop * loop;
            System.out.println("square of " + loop +
                        " is " + square);
            }
        }
    }
```

First, we declare an additional variable called square, in which we can save the current square number.

In the statement block, we use the loop variable in order to calculate the current square number. Imagine that we want to calculate the square numbers of the numbers 1 to 10. The loop variable, however, takes on the values 1 to 10 one after the other. So what seems more reasonable than to calculate the square number with the help of the loop variable?

We save the current square number in the variable square and then output this.

TIP

One could also have done without the intermediate storage in square. *The statement block would then have consisted of the following* println() *statement alone:*

```
System.out.println("square of " + loop + " is: "
        + (loop * loop));
```

To get used to programming with loops, the above code is surely easier to understand.

> **CAUTION**
>
> *While it is usual to query the value of the loop variable in the statement block of the loop and install the value in expression, you should strictly avoid changing the value in the loop variable in the statement block. The modification of the loop variable should only be carried out in the loop header.*

4 Save the program as `ForLoop.java`. Compile and execute it (Figure 9.1).

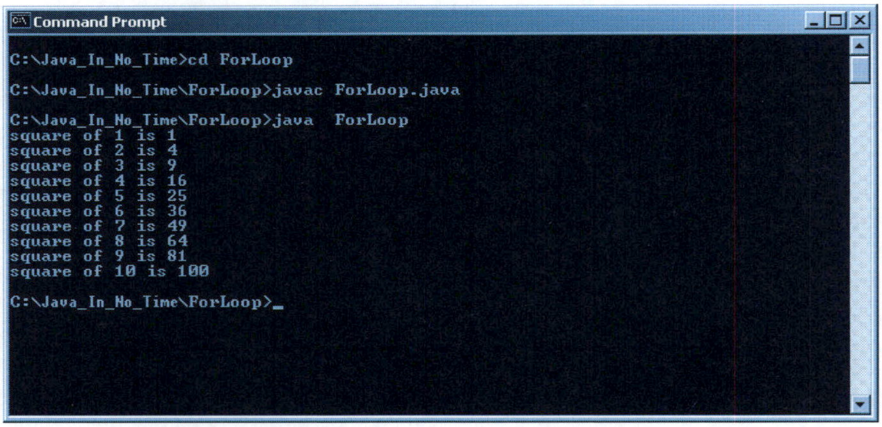

Command Prompt
C:\Java_In_No_Time>cd ForLoop
C:\Java_In_No_Time\ForLoop>javac ForLoop.java
C:\Java_In_No_Time\ForLoop>java ForLoop
square of 1 is 1
square of 2 is 4
square of 3 is 9
square of 4 is 16
square of 5 is 25
square of 6 is 36
square of 7 is 49
square of 8 is 64
square of 9 is 81
square of 10 is 100
C:\Java_In_No_Time\ForLoop>_

Figure 9.1: Output of the program ForLoop.

Variants and traps

Instead of incrementing the loop variable, you can also decrement it:

```
for(loop = 10; loop > 1; --loop)
```

or change it in any another way:

```
for(loop = 1; loop < 10; loop+=2)
```

In the same way that you always select the condition and alteration of the loop variable, it is also important that conditions are set clearly for the loop to be abandoned. Look at the following loop:

```
for(loop=1; loop <= 10; loop--)
  {
  ...
  }
```

Here, the loop variable `loop` is decremented after every loop passage. This means that it is reduced by 1. However, since the initial value 1 is less than 10, and becomes even less with the decrement, the disconnection criterion can never be fulfilled. We have an endless loop.

Such endless loops are a frequent example of logical errors within a syntactically correct program.

Now, try to write a program that outputs the first hundred square numbers with the help of a `for` loop. After every tenth square number, the program will stop and wait until the user presses the ⏎ key. A little tip: with the help of the modulus operator % you can determine with a single `if` condition whether the current loop passage is a multiple of 10. This task is not very easy. If you have problems email me at *dirklouis@cs.com* (of course, solutions and success stories would also be very welcome!).

The while loop

The second important loop variant is the `while` loop.

Common syntax

In the `while` loop `initialisation`, `condition` and `alteration` are not combined in the loop header, but are distributed over the code. They are usually used if the programmer does not know exactly how often the loops are to be passed.

The common syntax of the `while` loop looks like this:

```
Initialization;
while (condition)
    {
    statement(s) including alteration;
    }
```

We see an example of this in the next section.

Loops controlled by the user

The following program also calculates square numbers. However, it does not just output a particular number of square numbers, but also asks the user to what number the square needs to be calculated to.

What is special about the program is that the user does not have to call the program every time for calculating another square number. Instead, the

129

program asks the user to enter another number. We will carry this out using a `while` loop

If the user wants to exit the program, he/she has to give a value of `0`.

1 Create a new program, `WhileLoop.java`, and begin with the following basic framework:

```
// square numbers with while-loop
import java.lang.*;

public class WhileLoop
    {
    public static void main(String[] args)
        {
        }
    }
```

2 Add a loop variable that is initialized by one. Create a variable of the `Buffered Reader` type for the connection to the keyboard.

```
// square numbers with while loop
import java.lang.*;
import java.io.*;

public class WhileLoop
    {
    public static void main(String[] args)
                                    throws IOException
        {
        double input = 1;
        BufferedReader t = new BufferedReader(
                new InputStreamReader(System.in));
        }
```

We will use the `double` variable `input` to read into the data over the keyboard and also to check the loop. Therefore, we have called the variable `input` and not `loop`. You already know what needs to be done to read input from the keyboard, so we will not repeat the explanation.

3 Create the while loop.

```
// square numbers with while loop
import java.lang.*;
import java.io.*;

public class WhileLoop
    {
    public static void main(String[] args)
                                    throws IOException
        {
        double input = 1;
```

```
BufferedReader t = new BufferedReader(
                new InputStreamReader(System.in));

while (input != 0)
   {
   }
}
}
```

The `while` loops begin with the keyword `while`. The loop condition follows this in round brackets. If this condition is met, the statement block of the loop is executed. In the example, the loop is executed as long as the value of `input` is not equal to `0`. Because we show `input` with the value `1` in the loop, the condition is met at the beginning, and the loop is therefore executed at least once.

4 Create the statement block of the loop.

```
// square numbers with while-loop
import java.lang.*;
import java.io.*;

public class WhileLoop
    {
    public static void main(String[] args)
                                throws IOException
        {
        double input = 1;
        BufferedReader t = new BufferedReader(
                    new InputStreamReader(System.in));
        String inputString;

        while (input != 0)
        {
        System.out.print("please enter number (0 = End): ");

        inputString = t.readLine();
        input = Integer.parseInt(inputString);

        System.out.println("square of " + input +
                    " is " + (input*input));
        }
        }
    }
```

In the case of the `while` loop, the value of the loop variable (expressed more generally, the value of the variables that are adopted in the loop condition) is changed in the statement part of the loop. In this example, this is possible by assigning the keyboard input to the variables `input` (more precisely, the converted number value from the read character string `inputString`).

5 Save the program as `WhileLoop.java`. Compile and execute the program (Figure 9.2).

```
Command Prompt                                              _ □ X

C:\Java_In_No_Time\WhileLoop>javac WhileLoop.java

C:\Java_In_No_Time\WhileLoop>java  WhileLoop
please enter number (0 = End): 4
square of 4.0 is 16.0
please enter number (0 = End): 10
square of 10.0 is 100.0
please enter number (0 = End): -7
square of -7.0 is 49.0
please enter number (0 = End): 0
square of 0.0 is 0.0

C:\Java_In_No_Time\WhileLoop>
```

Figure 9.2: Output of the program WhileLoop.

Aborting loops prematurely

It is possible, with the help of special commands:

- to abort the current loop passage;
- to abort the whole loop.

Aborting loop passages

Why should you abort a loop passage prematurely? In lots of loops, there are variables other than loop variables. Maybe one of these variables takes on a value in a loop passage that prohibits the current loop passage from being executed any further. Or maybe there are values of the loop variable for which you don't want to execute the statement of the loop at all. Let's assume that you want to distribute the first ten square numbers, but not the square of 5.

This cannot be done with just the help of the statement in the loop header, unless you put two loops after each other.

With the help of the `continue` statement, which aborts the current loop passage, the realisation of this kind of loop is not a problem.

1 Begin a new program `ForLoop2.java` and type in the source text of the program `ForLoop.java`. Change the class name into `ForLoop2`.

```java
// square numbers with for loop
import java.lang.*;

public class ForLoop2
    {
    public static void main(String[] args)
        {
        int loop;
        int square;

        for(loop = 1; loop <= 10; ++loop)
          {
          square = loop * loop;
          System.out.println("square of "+ loop +
                    "is " + square);
          }

        }
    }
```

2 Using an `if` condition, check at the beginning of the loop whether the value of `loop` is equal to 5.

```java
// square numbers with for loop
import java.lang.*;

public class ForLoop2
    {
    public static void main(String[] args)
        {
        int loop;
        int square;

        for(loop = 1; loop <= 10; ++loop)
          {
          if (loop == 5)
            {
            }

          square = loop * loop;
          System.out.println("square of "+ loop +
                    "is" + square);

          }

        }
    }
```

133

3 If the `if` condition is met, execute the statement `continue`.

```java
// square numbers with for loop
import java.lang.*;

public class ForLoop2
    {
    public static void main(String[] args)
        {
        int loop;
        int square;

        for(loop = 1; loop <= 10; ++loop)
            {
            if (loop == 5)
                {
                continue;
                }

            square = loop * loop;
            System.out.println("square of" + loop +
                        " is " + square);
            }
        }
    }
```

4 Save the program as `ForLoop2.java`. Compile and execute it.

For the first four loop blocks, the statement passage is executed normally. At the start of the fifth block, the `if` condition produces `true` and the `continue` statement is executed under the `if` condition. The `continue` statement makes sure that the following statement is no longer executed in the loop block. Instead, the loop is continued with the last statement in the loop header (`++loop`) and the joining of the next loop passage.

> **NOTE**
>
> The `if` condition and the `continue` statement must not stand at the start of the statement block of the loop. They can stand in any other position in the statement block.

> **CAUTION**
>
> *It is important that the loop variable is also rounded up (or down, depending on the construction of the loop) for the loop passage that was aborted by* continue. *In* for *loop this is always done because the third statement in the loop header, which is responsible for the modification of the loop variable, is always executed at the end of every loop passage. In* while *loops, the modification of the loop variable is always carried in the statement block of the loop. Therefore you must make sure that the modification of the loop variable stands in front of the* continue *statement. Otherwise, the loop is appended to an endless loop, with considerable safety if the* continue *statement is executed.*

If you think this warning is not important, try to understand what happens during the execution of the following while loop (but do not program the loops afterwards, because the program will inevitably crash):

```
int loop;        //loopvariable
int square;

loop = 1;

while (loop <= 10)
    {
    if (loop == 5)
        continue;

    square = loop * loop;
    cout << "The square of "<< loop << "is: "
        << quadr << endl;

    ++loop;
    }
```

If loop has reached the value 5, it will always stay at five, because the increase will then always be skipped by the ++loop.

Aborting loops

The break statement is used essentially in the same way as the continue statement. It aborts not only the current loop passage, but also the whole of the loop.

The break statement is used mostly if you have to cancel tasks of the following form:

"Execute the following statements, until a certain event occurs."

This formulation can be used easily on our program in the calculation of the square numbers in Chapter 9.

"Always ask the user to input another number for which the square will be calculated until a 0 is input."

Using an endless loop and a break statement, the implementation of this program would then look like the following:

1 Create a new program, BreakDemo.java, and type in the WhileLoop.java source text. However, do not forget to modify the class name in BreakDemo.

```
// square numbers with while loop
import java.lang.*;
import java.io.*;

public class BreakDemo
    {
    public static void main(String[] args)
                                        throws IOException
        {
        double input = 1;        //loopvariable
        String inputString;
```

```
        BufferedReader t = new BufferedReader(
                        new InputStreamReader(System.in));

        while (input!= 0)
        {
        System.out.print("Please input number (0 = End): ");

        inputString = t.readLine();
        input = Integer.parseInt(inputString);

        System.out.println("square of "+ input + "is "
                        + (input*input));
        }
        }
    }
```

2 Convert the `while` loop into an endless loop.

```
// square numbers with while loop
import java.lang.*;
import java.io.*;

public class BreakDemo
    {
    public static void main(String[] args)
                                        throws IOException
        {
        double input = 1;          //loopvariable
        String inputString;

        BufferedReader t = new BufferedReader(
                        new InputStreamReader(System.in));

        while (true)
        {
        System.out.print("please enter number (0 = End): ");

        inputString = t.readLine();
        input = Integer.parseInt(inputString);

        System.out.println("square of " + input + " is "
                        + (input*input));
        }
        }
    }
```

Instead of a genuine loop condition, we simply input `true` in round brackets after `while`. The compiler only considers the event of a condition and this can only be one of the two boolean logic values `true`/`false`. By entering `true`, the loop condition is always accepted as being met. The loop is then executed.

3 Insert the break statement to exit the loop.

```java
// square numbers with while loop
import java.lang.*;
import java.io.*;

public class BreakDemo
    {
    public static void main(String[] args)
                                    throws IOException
        {
        double input = 1;          //loopsvariable
        String inputString;

        BufferedReader t = new BufferedReader(
                        new InputStreamReader(System.in));

        while (true)
        {
        System.out.print("please enter number (0 = End): ");

        inputString = t.readLine();
        input = Integer.parseInt(inputString);

        if(input == 0)
            break;

        System.out.println("square of " + input + " is "
                        + (input*input));
        }
        }
    }
```

After reading the user input, we check with an if condition whether the user has input a 0.

- If the user has entered a value that is not equal to 0, then the loop is executed normally.

- If the user has entered 0, then the break statement is executed and the loop is exited immediately.

4 Save the program as `BreakDemo.java`. compile the program and execute it (Figure 9.3).

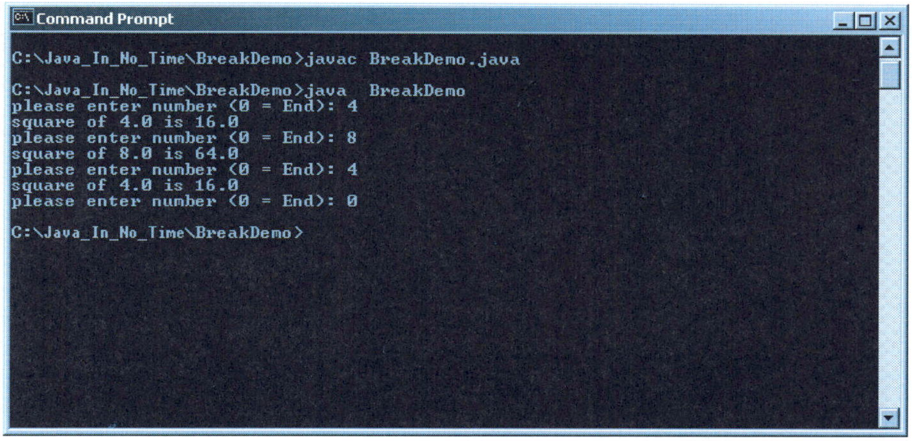

```
Command Prompt                                                    _ □ ×

C:\Java_In_No_Time\BreakDemo>javac BreakDemo.java

C:\Java_In_No_Time\BreakDemo>java  BreakDemo
please enter number (0 = End): 4
square of 4.0 is 16.0
please enter number (0 = End): 8
square of 8.0 is 64.0
please enter number (0 = End): 4
square of 4.0 is 16.0
please enter number (0 = End): 0

C:\Java_In_No_Time\BreakDemo>
```

Figure 9.3: Output of the program BreakDemo.

Chapter 10

Methods: bundling activities together

We have already learned about and used several predefined methods such as println(), sqrt(), tan() and also main(). In this chapter we will move our practical knowledge onto a sound theoretical base. Above all, we will learn how to define our own methods to solve specific programming problems.

Defining and calling methods

As you hopefully know, Java is an object-oriented programming language. The main mechanisms for conversion are classes, which we will explore in more detail in the next chapter. In this chapter, we will focus on a fundamental component – methods.

In a method, logically related activities (i.e. Java statements) are bundled together. A good example is the `println()` method of the class `System.out`. This contains all statements that are necessary to show a string submitted as parameter on the console.

There are many advantages of using methods, including:

- *a program is structured more easily and clearly, therefore it becomes more readable and easier to maintain;*

- *activities that are required repeatedly in the program have to be coded only once in the method, so you save time.*

To define a method, in principle, means nothing more than connecting a statement block that fulfils a specific task (for example, issues a text, or calculates the root of a number) with a name – the method name.

We will explain this with an example.

Defining methods

Our first method is going to produce a greeting to us. The code that will be contained in the method consists of a single `println()` statement:

```
System.out.println("Hello programmer!");
```

How does a method come from this statement?

1 Think up a name for the method and place round brackets after the name, which indicates that the name is a method name:

```
greeting()
```

This has to be entered inside the curved brackets of a class, and not outside. Methods always belong to a particular class.

2 Give the data type of the return value.

```
void greeting()
```

Methods can return result values. You can give the data type of the result (for example, `int`, `double` or `String`) before the function name. If the function does not return a result value, as in our example, you enter the keyword `void` instead of a data type.

WHAT IS THIS?

You can use the keyword `void` anywhere where the compiler expects a type input, or when you cannot or do not want to give a type. You already know this keyword from the numerous `main()` methods that we have drafted:

```
public static void main(String[] args)
```

Here, void means that the method main() returns no value.

3 Place the keyword `static` at the beginning if the method is to be called without an instance of the accompanying class.

```
static void greeting()
```

WHAT IS THIS?

The keyword `static` can precede a method in order to tell the compiler that this method will exist even if the class to which the method belongs does not exist as an instance during the running of the program, i.e. if there is no variable of the type of this class. In Chapter 13, you will learn more about this, and when you can leave `static` out.

You already know the keyword from the many `main()` methods: `public static void main(String[] args)`. The method has to be defined as `static` since it has been called as the first method at the start of the program. At this point, no class variables can be created.

4 Add a statement block after the method name.

```
static void greeting()
  {
  }
```

5 Draft the code that is to be executed when the method is called.

```
static void greeting()
  {
  System.out.println("Hello programmer!");
  }
```

Calling methods

In order to call the method `greeting()`, you need to type the full method name (including the round brackets) in the code at the place at which the method is to be executed. The full method name means the name of the class to which the method belongs, followed by a dot and the actual class name. Look at `System.out.println()`. The class is `System.out`, and the method itself is called `println()`. The keywords that preceed the definition (such as `void` or `static`) can no longer be entered in the call.

A slight simplification arises if a method is called within a class in which it is defined. For example, if the `System.out` class is called in your own `println()` method in your code, then you just have to enter `println()` and not the full name `System.out.println()` (although this is also possible).

1 Create a new program, `greeting.java`, and begin with the usual basic framework:

```
// Class with greeting method
public class greeting
  {
    public static void main(String[] args)
      {
      }
  }
```

2 Define a method `greeting()` before or after the `main()` method, but within the class `greeting`.

```
// class with greeting method
public class greeting
    {
    public static void main(String[] args)
        {
        }

    void greeting()
        {
        System.out.println("Hello programmer!");
        }
    }
```

3 Call the method greeting() as the first statement in main().

```
// Class with greeting method
public class greeting
    {
    public static void main(String[] args)
        {
        greeting();
        }

    static void greeting()
        {
        System.out.println("Hello programmer!");
        }
    }
```

4 Then add a println() entry followed by a renewed call of greeting():

```
// class with greeting method
public class greeting
    {
    public static void main(String[] args)
        {
        greeting();
        System.out.println("greeting of main()");
        greeting();
        }

    static void greeting()
        {
        System.out.println("Hello programmer!");
        }

    }
```

5 Save the program as greeting.java, compile and execute it (Figure 10.1).

Figure 10.1: Output of the greeting *program.*

Advantages of methods

Bundling logical methods that belong together has many advantages.

One advantage is that the code is structured more clearly. Imagine that you have to write a program that reads measurements from a file and outputs them as a table as well as a graph. This kind of a program can lead to some hundred lines of code. If you divide up the code into methods (one method to read data, one to create the table and one for the graph), the program stays clear:

```java
static void feed_data()
   {
   ...
   }

static void create_table()
   {
   ...
   }

static void create_graph()
   {
   ...
   }

public static void main(String[] args)
   {
   read_data();
   create_table();
```

```
   create_graph();
   }
```

Another advantage is that you can carry out alterations or corrections more easily. Imagine that you want to change the greeting formula of the program in the example above, so that the program welcomes you with your name, `"Hello Jenni!"` for instance. You have just to adapt the code of the method `greeting()`:

```
static void greeting()
   {
   System.out.println("Hello Jenni!");
   }
```

If we had not defined a method, we would have had to go through all the places in the code where the greeting is given and change the greeting formula every time – a tedious method that is prone to faults.

Finally, you can also use methods that have already been defined in other programs without problems. We have already done this with the method `println()` of the class `System.out`.

Submitting parameters to methods

Our method `greeting()`, defined in the section above, is extremely uncommunicative as it does not allow any exchange of data between itself and the code to be called. However, lots of methods become really valuable when they take on data that have to be processed from the caller and possibly even return result values. We already know the process from the methods such as `println()`, `sqrt()`, `tan()` etc., which are defined in the different packages.

Parameters and arguments

If a method is to take on a value during the call, you have to give a variable for this value in the method definition in round brackets.

Let's look at our greeting function again.

```
static void greeting()
   {
   System.out.println("Hello programmer!");
   }
```

This method would be more versatile if you could submit the name of the person you want to welcome to the function as an argument.

1 Define a parameter of the String type for the method.

```
static void greeting(String name)
   {
   System.out.println("Hello programmer!");
   }
```

2 Use the parameter in the statement block of the method.

```
static void greeting(String name)
   {
   System.out.println("Hello " + name);
   }
```

3 Call the method using an argument.

```
public static void main(String[] args)
   {
   ...
   greeting("Jonathan");
   ...
   greeting("Melanie");
   ...
```

It is important that the type of the argument matches the type of the parameter.

In this way, we can demystify the method head of the `main()` method further:

```
public static void main(String[] args)
```

During the call, `main()` also apparently expects a parameter to do with `String`. We will go into more detail about `[]` later. It means that a *field of strings* is submitted.

But since `main()` is not called inside our Java program, but by the runtime environment, we do not have to concern ourselves with this parameter.

Several parameters

A method can also submit several parameters. Parameters can have different data types, and they are listed one after the other in round brackets (data type and name, respectively) and separated with commas.

```
static void demo (string par1, int par2, int par3)
  {
  here the statement(s);
  }
```

When the method is called, the suitable arguments are submitted to the parameters, separated with commas and in the same order.

```
demo("Text", 12, 4940);
```

In doing this, it is important that the sequence of the argument and its data types correspond to the method definition. Therefore you cannot call

```
demo(12, 4940,"Text");
```

or the compiler would complain.

Returning values from methods

It is as easy to submit a value as a method as it is to return a value from the method.

For example, let's take a look at the following function that calculates the square of the argument you have submitted.

```
static void square (int number);
  {
  int result;
  result = number * number;

  System.out.println(result);
  }
```

Call:

```
int value = 12;
square(value);        // output: 144
```

Instead of outputting the calculated result on the console, the function will be written so that the result is returned to the caller.

1 Give the data type of the result value in the method definition. Since we return an int value, we replace the type input void with int.

```
static int square (int number);
  {
  int result;
  result = number * number;

  System.out.println(result);
  }
```

2 Return the result value to the caller at the end of the statement block of the method by means of the `return` keyword.

```
static int square (int number);
  {
  int result;
  result = number * number;

  return result;
  }
```

We have removed the output statement from the method. The part of the program to be called (e.g. the `main()` method) has to take care of the further processing.

3 Accept the result value in the call of the method.

```
int value = 12;
int result;

result = square(value);
```

4 Output the result.

```
int value = 12;
int result;

result = square(value);

System.out.println(result);
```

Several return statements

A function can always return a value as a return value. This does not mean, however, that it can only contain one `return` statement. A function can contain several `return` statements; for example, it can return different return values depending on the `if` condition.

```
boolean demo()
  {
  ...
  if(condition)
    {
      ...
     return true;
    }
    else
    {
      ...
     return false;
    }
  }
```

Modularisation using methods

In order to gain some more practical experience with methods, let's go back to the Fahrenheit3.java code from Chapter 7 and try to rewrite the program so that we can carry out the conversion from Fahrenheit to centigrade by means of a separate method.

1 Create a new program, Fahrenheit4.java, and type in the code of Fahrenheit3.java. Change the class name to Fahrenheit4.

```
// Fahrenheit conversion 4. Version
import java.lang.*;
import java.io.*;

public class Fahrenheit4
    {
    public static void main(String[] args)
                                    throws IOException
        {
        double fahrenheit;
        double centigrade;

        System.out.print("Temperature in Fahrenheit: ");

        // connection with the keyboard
        BufferedReader t = new BufferedReader(
                    new InputStreamReader(System.in));
        String input = t.readLine();

        fahrenheit = Double.parseDouble(input);

        centigrade = (fahrenheit - 32) * 5.0 / 9.0;

        int temp = (int) (centigrade * 100.0);

        centigrade = temp / 100.0;
```

```
        System.out.println(fahrenheit +
                        " degree Fahrenheit correspond to");
        System.out.println( centigrade + " degree centi-
grade");
        }
    }
```

2 Before the `main()` method, define a new method, `centigrade()`, that takes on a double parameter for taking on the Fahrenheit value and returns the calculated centigrade value as a `double` value.

```
// Fahrenheit  conversion 4. Version

import java.lang.*;
import java.io.*;

public class Fahrenheit4
    {
    static double centigrade(double fahrenheit)
        {
        }

  public static void main(String[] args)
                                throws IOException
        {
        double fahrenheit;
        double centigrade;

        System.out.print("Temperature in Fahrenheit: ");

        // connection with the keyboard
        BufferedReader t = new BufferedReader(
                        new InputStreamReader(System.in));
        String input = t.readLine();

        fahrenheit = Double.parseDouble(input);

        centigrade = (fahrenheit - 32) * 5.0 / 9.0;

        int temp = (int) (centigrade * 100.0);

        centigrade = temp / 100.0;

        System.out.println(fahrenheit +
                        " degree Fahrenheit correspond to ");
        System.out.println( centigrade + " degree centi-
grade");
        }
    }
```

3 Transfer the code for the calculation of the centigrade value from the `main()` function to `centigrade()` and return the calculated centigrade value.

```java
// Fahrenheit conversion 4. Version
import java.lang.*;
import java.io.*;

public class Fahrenheit4
    {
    static double centigrade(double fahrenheit)
        {

        double centigrade = (fahrenheit - 32) * 5.0 / 9.0;

        int temp = (int) (centigrade * 100.0);
        centigrade = temp / 100.0;

        return centigrade;

        }

  public static void main(String[] args)
                                    throws IOException

        {
        double fahrenheit;

        System.out.print("Temperature in Fahrenheit: ");

        // connection with the keyboard
        BufferedReader t = new BufferedReader(
                    new InputStreamReader(System.in));

        String input = t.readLine();

        fahrenheit = Double.parseDouble(input);


        System.out.println(fahrenheit +
                    " degree Fahrenheit correspond to ");

        System.out.println( centigrade + " degree centi-
grade");
        }
    }
```

4 Call the method `centigrade()` in `main()`.

```
// Fahrenheit conversion 4. Version
import java.lang.*;
import java.io.*;
public class Fahrenheit4
    {
    static double centigrade(double fahrenheit)
        {
        double centigrade = (fahrenheit - 32) * 5.0 / 9.0;

        int temp = (int) (centigrade * 100.0);
        centigrade = temp / 100.0;

        return centigrade;
        }

 public static void main(String[] args)
                                    throws IOException
        {
        double fahrenheit;
        double centigrade;

        System.out.print("Temperature in Fahrenheit: ");

        // connection with the keyboard
        BufferedReader t = new BufferedReader(
                        new InputStreamReader(System.in));
        String input = t.readLine();

        fahrenheit = Double.parseDouble(input);
        centigrade = centigrade(fahrenheit);
        System.out.println(fahrenheit +
                        " degree Fahrenheit correspond to ");
        System.out.println( centigrade + " degree centi-
grade");
        }
    }
```

NOTE

You can install methods that return a value in the same way as variables in expressions. In the example above, we would have saved the variable `centigrade` inside `main()` and been able to add the method call of `centigrade()` directly to `println()`:

```
System.out.println(fahrenheit +
                    " degree Fahrenheit correspond to
");

System.out.println( centigrade(fahrenheit) +
                    " degree centigrade");
```

5 Save the program as `Fahrenheit4.java`. Compile and execute it (Figure 10.2).

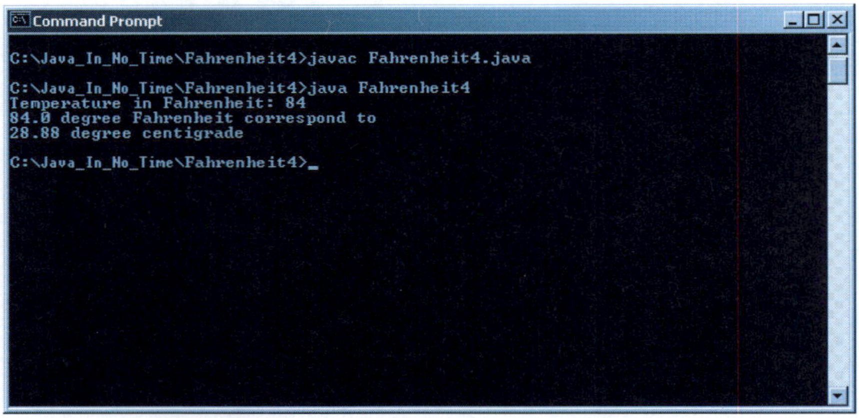

Figure 10.2: Output of the Fahrenheit4 *program.*

Scope of the variables

In the previous example, you may have wondered whether there was any problem because the variables `fahrenheit` and `centigrade` occur twice: they are defined in `main()` and in the `centigrade()` methods (in `centigrade()`, the variable `centigrade` is a normal variable and the variable `fahrenheit` is a parameter variable).

If you have compiled and executed the program, you will know that this does not cause any problems. The reason is that variables are always only valid in the method in which they are defined. These are also called *local variables*. Outside of the method, a local variable is not visible and therefore cannot be used. The reverse of this means that any possible similarities in the names do not interfere with anything. The same happens for the parameter of a method (which, in principle, can be understood as the local variable of the respective method).

In addition to this, there are also variables that are defined outside of a method (particularly outside of the `main()` method). These kinds of variables are called class or instance variables.[1] As a rule, they are normally valid and

---

1. There is a subtle difference between the two concepts, but we will not consider it in this book.

visible, and can be used by any method of the class. We will look at this in more detail in Chapter 13.

> **TIP**
>
> *At this point, you may be tempted to simply make all variables class variables outside of the method. This may seem practical as you would not need to exchange data between methods over parameters because everything could be done with the same variables.*
>
> *But trust us: this makes your program prone to errors, as well as making it almost unreadable.*

Common syntax of methods

To conclude, we will now show you the general syntax of a method definition:

```
static return type function name (parameter list)
   {
   statement(s);
   }
```

Chapter 11

Arrays – processing 1000 data elements at the same time

Until now, we have processed only single data items: individual integer values, floating-point numbers or strings. However, what do you need to do if you have a hundred or even a thousand values at the same time in a program? Do you really have to explicitly declare and process all those variables? Luckily, you don't have to, because for processing larger collections of data of a common data type, you can fall back on the concept of arrays.

Declaring arrays

Arrays are data structures that are defined by the programmer and in which you can give several variable of a data type. For example, assume that you need 100 integer variables to save 100 measurement values. Declaring a hundred integer variables explicitly would be an unnecessary and long-winded task:

```
int i1;
int i2;
...
```

Arrays make it possible to define any number of variables of the same data type in a block. Let's see how we can achieve it:

1 Create a new program, `mean_average_value.java` and begin with the following basic framework:

```
// mean average value calculation
import java.lang.*;
import java.io.*;

public class mean_average_value
    {
    public static void main(String[] args)
                                    throws IOException

        {

        }
    }
```

Then declare an array for `double` values.

2 Give the data type and the name of the array.

```
// mean average calculation
import java.lang.*;
import java.io.*;

public class mean_average_value
    {
    public static void main(String[] args)
                                    throws IOException

        {
        double[] measurements;
        }
    }
```

The declaration of an array consists of the data type followed by `[]` and the name of the array. The square brackets tell the compiler that this is an array and not a single `double` variable.

With this step, the array has not yet been assigned any memory (unlike the normal variable declaration), which means that the array is not ready to operate.

3 Assign memory to the array.

```
// mean average calculation
import java.lang.*;
import java.io.*;

public class mean_average_value
   {
   public static void main(String[] args)
                              throws IOException
     {
     double[] measurement;

     measurement = new double[10];
      }
   }
```

The number of the elements in the array is shown to the compiler by the expression of the form of the array variable

```
new data type [number]
```

In the example, we have the data type `double`, and the number is `10`.

The keyword `new` is a special operator, which we will meet again when dealing with the creation of class instances in Chapter12.

Accessing array elements

The elements of an array are stored behind each other in the memory as a block (see Figure 11.1). This makes it possible for the programmer to identify the individual elements in array by their position in the array. The position is appended to the array name as an index in square brackets. However, notice that the numbering of the elements in array begins with 0, and the first element in array therefore has the index 0.

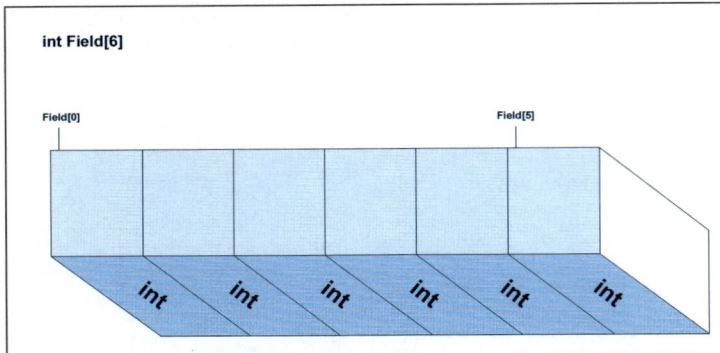

int Field[6]

Field[0]

Field[5]

int   int   int   int   int   int

Figure 11.1: An int *array in the memory.*

For clarification, we will now assign a value to the first element in the array
measurement.

1 Enter a value using the keyboard.

```
// mean average calculation

import java.lang.*;
import java.io.*;

public class mean_average_value
    {
    public static void main(String[] args)
                                        throws IOException
        {
        double[] measurement;
        measurement = new double[10];

        BufferedReader t = new BufferedReader(
                new InputStreamReader(System.in));

        String input;
        int temp;

        System.out.print("Measurement: ");

        input = t.readLine();
        temp = Integer.parseInt(input);

        }
    }
```

2 Assign the entered value to the first element in the array.

```
// mean average calculation

import java.lang.*;
import java.io.*;

public class mean_average_value
    {
    public static void main(String[] args)
                                throws IOException
        {
        double[] measurement;
        measurement = new double[10];
        BufferedReader t = new BufferedReader(
                new InputStreamReader(System.in));

        String input;
        int temp;

        System.out.print("measurement: ");
        input = t.readLine();
        temp = Integer.parseInt(input);

        measurement[0] = temp;

        }
    }
```

The access to an element in the array seems similar to the declaration of the array. The only difference is that the square brackets are not left blank but contain the index of the corresponding element.

> **CAUTION**
>
> *The first element in the array has the index 0. The last index is the number of the element in the array minus 1.*

Arrays in loops

Using loops, you can easily process any large array element by element. The loop variable is normally used as an index for the access to the elements.

We will use this to initialise our array.

1 Create a `for` loop that runs from 0 to 9.

```java
// mean average calculation
import java.lang.*;
import java.io.*;

public class mean_average
    {
    public static void main(String[] args)
                                    throws IOException
        {
        double[] measurement;
        measurement = new double[10];
        BufferedReader t = new BufferedReader(
                new InputStreamReader(System.in));
        String input;
        int temp,loop;

        System.out.print("measurement: ");
        input = t.readLine();
        temp = Integer.parseInt(input);

        for(loop = 0; loop <= 9; ++loop)
          {
          }
        }
    }
```

Notice that in an array containing ten elements the index runs from 0 to 9.

CAUTION

The last element in an array containing n elements has index n–1. Any access of over n–1 would lead to the program being aborted by the Java runtime environment.

NOTE

If the number of the elements of an array is not known, `length` *helps you; each array that has saved the number of the entries possesses this variable. The access is carried using the point operator, e.g.* `nt number = measurement.length`

2 Move the statement for the reading of a value from the keyboard to inside the loop.

```
// mean average calculation
import java.lang.*;
import java.io.*;

public class mean_average
    {
    public static void main(String[] args)
                                    throws IOException
        {
        double[] measurement;

        measurement = new double[10];
        BufferedReader t = new BufferedReader(
                new InputStreamReader(System.in));
        String input;
        int temp,loop;


        for(loop = 0; loop <= 9; ++loop)
          {
          System.out.print("measurement: ");
          input = t.readLine();
          temp = Integer.parseInt(input);
          }
      }
    }
```

3 Assign the values that have been read to the array elements, one after the other.

```
// mean average calculation
import java.lang.*;
import java.io.*;

public class mean_average
    {
    public static void main(String[] args)
                                    throws IOException
        {
        double[] measurement;
        measurement = new double[10];
        BufferedReader t = new BufferedReader(
                new InputStreamReader(System.in));
        String input;
        int temp,loop;

        for(loop = 0; loop <= 9; ++loop)
          {
          System.out.print("measurement: ");
          input = t.readLine();
          temp = Integer.parseInt(input);
```

```
          measurement[loop] = temp;
          }
      }
  }
```

In order to access the next element in the array automatically with every new loop passage, we simply use the loop variable `loop` just as index.

4 Calculate the mean average of the value in a second loop and output it.

```java
// mean averagecalculation
import java.lang.*;
import java.io.*;

public class mean_average
    {
    public static void main(String[] args)
                                    throws IOException
        {
        double[] measurement;
        measurement = new double[10];
        BufferedReader t = new BufferedReader(
                new InputStreamReader(System.in));
        String input;
        int temp,loop;

        for(loop = 0; loop <= 9; ++loop)
          {
          System.out.print("measurement: ");

          input = t.readLine();
          temp = Integer.parseInt(input);

          measurement[loop] = temp;
          }

        double mean_average = 0;

        for(loop = 0; loop <= 9; ++loop)
          {
          mean_average += measurement[loop];
          }

        mean_average = mean_average / 10.0;
        System.out.println("mean average = " +
                        mean_average);
        }
    }
```

We calculate the mean average using a `double` variable with the same name that we declare at the beginning and initialise with the value 0.

We add the array values one after the other to the respective last value of the variable `mean average` in a loop used for reading.

Finally, the mean average (sum of the values/ number of the values) is output.

5 Save the program as `mean_average.java`. Compile and execute it (Figure 11.2).

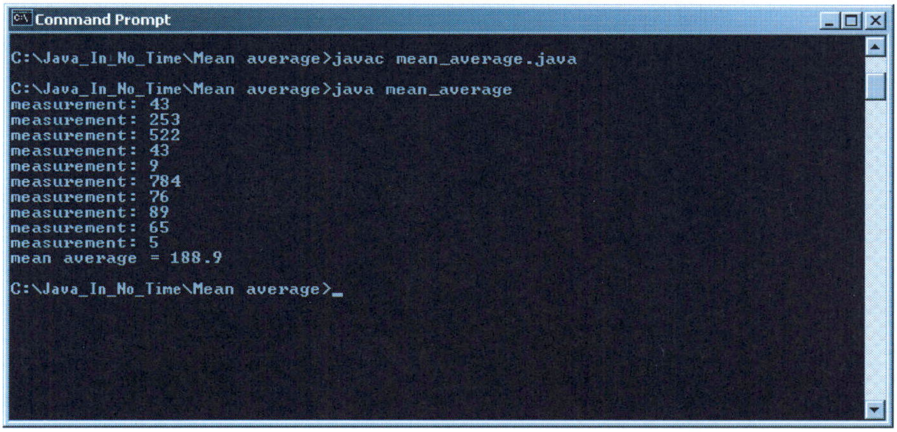

```
C:\Java_In_No_Time\Mean average>javac mean_average.java

C:\Java_In_No_Time\Mean average>java mean_average
measurement: 43
measurement: 253
measurement: 522
measurement: 43
measurement: 9
measurement: 784
measurement: 76
measurement: 89
measurement: 65
measurement: 5
mean average = 188.9

C:\Java_In_No_Time\Mean average>_
```

Figure 11.2: Output of the mean average *program.*

Chapter 12

The object-oriented revolution

"Object-oriented programming" is one of the biggest catchwords that has characterised the programming scene of the last few years. The world is seen as a collection of objects, and this view is reflected also in a programming language. We will find out about this basic idea in this chapter.

Thinking object-oriented

The techniques of object-oriented programming aim, amongst other things, to make the source code clearer, more modular, and safer and reusable.The trick that object-oriented programming uses is to combine related data and activities (i.e. methods), which operate on the data, into objects.

Let's assume that you are writing a program for the management of a bank account. Different data belong to the bank account:

- name of the account holder
- account number
- balance
- credit

Furthermore, there are different operations that are carried out on the bank account:

- balance query
- deposits
- withdrawals

Without object-oriented concepts, the bank account is represented in your program by means of a collection of individual variables (for the data) and methods (for the operations on the data). The connection between these data and methods is in your head. However, the problem is that you have to keep an overview of which methods can be used, on which data, and in which order. Let's assume we are dealing with a large program created for a bank that does not manage just one account, but also the accounts of all customers, plus customers' data, bookings that are carried out, credit given, etc. You end up with a heap of data and methods, and your task is to remember when you can call which methods for which data.

Object-oriented programming starts here. It sees customers, accounts, bookings and credits as objects. All of these objects have their own variables and methods. Objects that contain the same variables and methods (e.g. all accounts) belong to a general class (in this case, the class of the accounts).

For the programmer, this has the advantage that he/she can think in objects instead of individual data and functions. If programmers wish to raise the balance of a particular account, they do not need to know what the variable is called, where the balance of the account is stored, or what method is used to make deposits. They simply call the pay method of the account object.

Containing data and methods in classes is the basis of object-oriented programming on which further concepts are built up (protection mechanisms for classes, inheritance, polymorphism, templates, etc.) All these concepts aim to organise the source code better, in order to make the creation of the code easier, as well as simplifying its maintenance and possible reutilisation. It is obvious that these concepts prove more beneficial the more extensive the code is and the more various types of data are processed in the code.

The class as a basis

Object-oriented programming is based on the concept of the class – a concept that can be approached in two different ways:

- through the "philosophy" of object-oriented programming;
- through seeeing the class as a new data type.

During programming, you always need to have both aspects at the back of your mind. In the planning stage, when you conceive your program and work on ideas, you will see your classes as pure data types.

A simple example should clarify all this.

Planning and converting a program to calculate vectors

Let's assume that you are to write a program with which you can add two dimensional vectors. How do you do this?

1 Identify the classes and objects that the program is to process.

Classes and objects

The relationship between class and object should be clear.

In the object-oriented conceptual model, an object is a real thing, for example, you, your neighbour, the pencil that is in your hand, or the trees that you can see if you look out of the window. On the one hand, each of these objects is unique; on the other hand, for each of these objects, there is also a similar object. If, for example, you go into a stationery shop to buy a coloured pencil, you will find red, blue, green and yellow, thick and thin, and cheap and expensive pencils.

In order to describe similar objects, we use generic terms: "coloured pencil", for example, is a generic term. It creates the idea of a long, thin wooden writing implement that has a particular colour and thickness, and that can be sharpened and used to draw with. Notice that the term "coloured pencil" does not say anything about the exact colour or thickness: it only establishes that the object that we see as a coloured pencil has a colour and a thickness. The colour and thickness of a coloured pencil object is a different thing.

In object-oriented programming, a generic term is called "class object". Classes are also common descriptions for a group of similar objects. However, while we normally only use generic terms in natural languages to describe and classify objects that we encounter in our daily life, in object-oriented programming, classes accomplish two tasks:

- they describe the things that we want to use in the program;
- they serve as patterns or moulds from which we create the objects that we want to work with.

In the program required for the vectorial addition, we find just one class of objects: two-dimensional vectors.

2 Set the qualities and method of the object.

In the two-dimensional space, vectors are defined by an x and a y value. You can therefore also see a vector as an arrow that points to a point (x, y) from the origin of the coordination system (Figure 12.1).

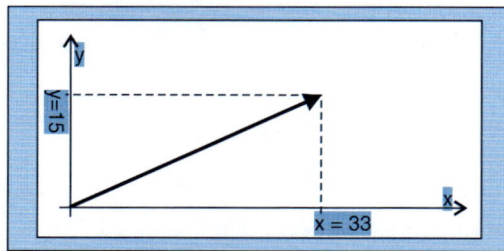

Figure 12.1: A vector as two-dimensional coordinate.

Every vector has at least two properties: an x and a y coordinate. We can take on even more properties, for example the length of the vector, but for the moment, the x and the y coordinates are sufficient.

The method of the vectors are the operations that we want to execute. For our program, we simply need an operation for the addition of the vectors (Figure 12.2).

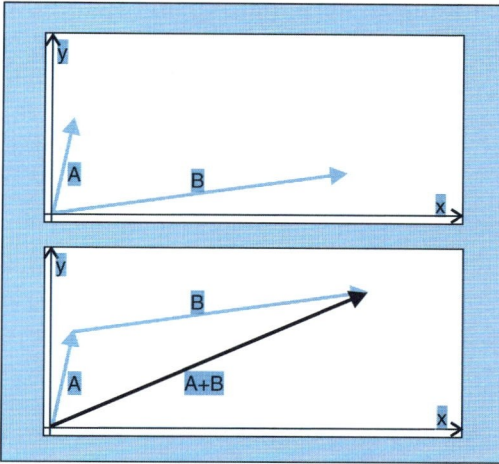

Figure 12.2: Vector addition.

Other methods that are not of interest to us here include subtraction, the calculation of the scalar outcome, the calculation of the vector outcome, and the calculation of the length.

> **WHAT IS THIS?**
>
> *Classes describe objects using* properties *and methods.*
>
> *The* properties *of a class* `colour pencil` *would, for example, be colour and thickness. The* methods *are the activities that the objects of the class can carry out, for example the operations that we want to use when programming objects of the class.*

Of course, real objects normally have so many properties and methods that is impossible for us to copy them all into one class definition. You can also select the properties and methods that are interesting when programming with the objects of the class.

3 Change the general description of the `vector` class in a Java class definition.

Obviously, this is not very easy for a beginner who has never defined his own class. You already know from the previous chapter that there is the keyword `class` for this purpose. Here we are satisfied with an outline of the class `vector`. We are not interested in the exact syntax of the class definition (yet).

e moment, we are dealing with the basic principle, and with how
erties and methods influence the class definition.

```
ss vector

    / The properties
    .nt x;
    int y;

    // The behaviours
    void add_up(vector v);
      {
      x += v.x;
      y += v.y;
      }
    }
```

As you can see, properties are defined as variables in the class and
behaviours as methods.

4 Classes are used in the program by a variable of its type being created (defined
as *instance*).

```
// class Demo
import java.lang.*;

class vector
    {
    // The properties
    int x;
    int y;

    // The behaviours
    void add_up(vector v)
      {
      x += v.x;
```

```
      y += v.y;
      }

  }

public class ClassesDemo
    {
    public static void main(String[] args)
        {
        vector v1 = new vector();
        vector v2 = new vector();
        }
    }
```

In the `main()` method of the frame `ClassDemo`, two instances of our class `vector` are defined. This is carried out by means of the `new` operator that you already know from the creation of arrays.

WHAT IS THIS?

There is a name for the variables of class types: they are called instances. *Therefore, the declaration of a variable of the type of the class is also called* instance formation *or* instancing. *For the instancing of classes, the* `new` *operator is used as follows:*

```
Class name = new Class();
```

The following occurs during instance formation:

- An object of the class is created. This object exists as memory area in the working memory of the computer. It contains space for the instance variables defined in the class.

- The compiler calls a particular class method: the *constructor*. The constructor always has the same name as the accompanying class. Therefore, in our example it is called `vector()` (the `()` belongs to it, as it is a method).

- The task of the constructor is to check whether the created object is correctly initialized. If you do not draft a constructor (as in the example), the compiler internally creates a standard constructor for the class. If you want to use the instance variable for the initialization, you have to draft your own constructor (see Chapter 13).

The created object is combined with the assigned variable (in the example `v1` or `v2`). From now on, the Java program can access the objects using the variable name.

5 Program with the objects of the class.

```java
// ClassDemo
import java.lang.*;

class vector
   {
   // The properties
   int x;
   int y;

   // The behaviours
   void add_up(vector v)
      {
      x += v.x;
      y += v.y;
      }
   }

public class ClassDemo
   {
   public static void main(String[] args)
      {
      vector v1 = new vector();
      vector v2 = new vector();

      v1.x = 10;
      v1.y = 25;

      v2.x = 10;
      v2.y = -20;

      v1.add_up(v2);

      System.out.println("v1.x = " + v1.x);
      System.out.println("v1.y = " + v1.y);

      }
   }
```

In the program, objects are represented by the affiliated instances. All of these instances have their own set of instance variables (as they are defined in the class) and for each of these instances we can call the methods defined in the class. Access to properties and methods is always carried out using the instance name and the dot operator.

> **CAUTION**
>
> *It is not entirely correct to say that you can access all properties and methods defined in the class using the instance name. You can access by means of the modifiers* `public`, `private` *or* `protected`. *We will look at this in more in detail in Chapter 13.*

6 Save the program as `ClassesDemo.java`. Compile and execute it (Figure 12.3).

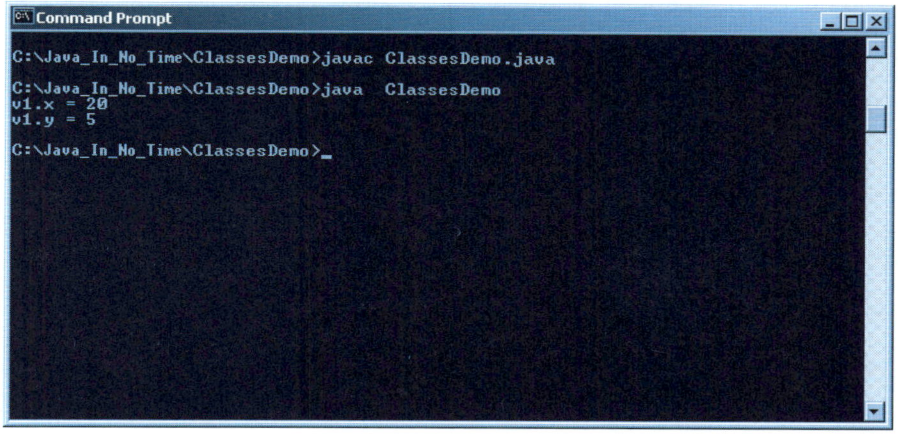

Figure 12.3: Output of the program ClassDemo.

A basic lesson

After the limited overview of the fundamental concepts "object" and "class", we now want to take a look at the definition and the use of classes.

The definition of a class consists of the following components:

- the class name
- the properties (= instance variables)
- the methods
- the constructor

In order to grasp the meaning of these single components of a class definition, you always need to look at the class from two different points of view:

- from the point of view of the programmer who defines the class;
- from the point of view of the programmer who uses the class by creating and using the objects of this class in its programs.

It does not matter that we usually embody both roles. It is important that when defining a class, we should remember that someone later will have to use our class to program with. And this person rightly expects to program *meaningfully, easily* and *safely* with the objects of the class.

With this in mind, we now want to pursue, step by step, how a class is drafted for a two-dimensional vector, i.e. we show the input example you already know from above. This will partly show repetition. In this chapter, you will learn more details about the single elements of a class definition, and see how this becomes a valid and operating class. In the following chapter, you will learn more information regarding advanced aspects.

1 Create a new program `vectorcalculation.java`, and begin with the following basic framework:

```
// vector calculation
import java.lang.*;

public class vectorCalculation
    {
    public static void main(String[] args)
        {
        }
    }
```

The following step consists in setting up the basic framework for the class `vector`.

The class framework

The common syntax of a class definition appears a follows:

```
class classname
    {
    // Elements
    }
```

The definition starts with the keyword `class`, which shows the compiler that a class definition now follows.

The name of the class, which you can choose, follows the keyword `class` (according to the general rules for naming; as well as this, class names usually began with a capital letter).

The elements of the class are listed in curly brackets.

> **NOTE**
>
> *If you look at the code for larger programs, you will occasionally come across class definitions in which the keyword* extends *follows the class name, followed by a further class name. This is the instruction of a basic class. In this case, the newly defined class automatically receives all the elements of the entered basic class. We call this inheritance – it is a very important concept in object-oriented programming, but for now we will leave this to the more experienced programmers.*

If you compare these explanations for the setup of a class with the above basic framework of the class vectorCalculation, you will notice that the keyword public still appears before class. This is a *modifier* or an *access specificator*, which establishes who (in the sense of which other class) can access this class and its components. We will look at this in more detail later.

2 Create a class definition for the class vector.

```
// vector calculation
import java.lang.*;

public class vectorcalculation
    {
  public static void main(String[] args)
        {
        }
    }

class vector
    {
    }
```

Notice that we define the new class vector outside the class vectorcalculation (we could also define this inside of it, but in doing so, we would get a special *inner class,* which would go beyond the scope of this introduction) and that it is defined as public without an access specificator. There are two good reasons for this. First, up to now you have learned hardly anything about this access specificator, and second, the frame class vectorCalculation has already been defined as public. You should notice:

Properties

The properties, i.e. the data of the class, are defined in the class as normal variables. Just remember that they are defined outside of the method in brackets {}. It does not matter where they are placed, but they are usually at the beginning.

3 Define the instance variables for the `vector` class.

```
// vector calculation
import java.lang.*;

public class vectorcalculation
   {
   public static void main(String[] args)
      {
      }
   }

class vector
   {
   // Instance variables
   double x;
   double y;
   }
```

The properties that have to be included in a class definition cannot always be established as easily in our vector example. It is then better to weigh up which properties are important and which are unimportant, or even nonsensical.

Let's look at other possible properties for our `vector` class:

- A `colour` property is neither a characteristic property for a vector nor a property that we can use to implement vectors – therefore we do without it.

- Things look different with the properties `length` and `angle`. You can define vectors not only by entering the *x* and *y* coordinates but also by entering an angle (calculated from the horizontal line) and a length. `Length` and `angle` are quite realistic and possibly useful properties. Nevertheless, at the moment, we will do without these properties, since in our program we want to focus on the representation of the vectorial coordinates.

The instance variables have now been defined; the question we are now asking ourselves is how to work with them, i.e. which activities (methods) do we want to provide?

Methods

Methods establish what you can do with the objects of the class. If you are not sure which methods have to be included in a class definition, ask yourself the following questions:

- What do you normally do in the real world with objects that represent my class?

- What will the programmers who use my class do with the objects of the class?

- What do I want to use my own class for, and what do I want to do with the objects of the class?

In our example, the program will calculate using vectors. For instance, typical activities are addition, subtraction, scalar outcome, etc. Since the results of the program have to be output, perhaps a method for the output of vectors would be practical.

4 Define the methods required for the `vector` class.

```java
// vector calculation
import java.lang.*;

public class vectorcalculation
    {
  public static void main(String[] args)
        {
        }
    }

class vector
    {
    // Instance variables
    double x;
    double y;

    // Methods
    void addUp(vector v)
      {
      x += v.x;
      y += v.y;
      }
    void distribute()
      {
      System.out.println("(" + x + "," + y + ")");
      }
    }
```

To the many conceivable methods, we have added two methods: `add up()` and `output()`. You may be wondering why the method `add up()`, which has to add two more vectors, still contains a vector as argument, and why it does not return the result of the addition as return value. What does it mean that both methods access the data elements `x` and `y`? To answer these questions, we have to explore further afield.

If you draft methods for classes, you have to also take into account that methods are always called by the instances of the class:[1]

```java
vector vect1, vect2;

addUp(vect2). vect1.;
vect1. distribute();
```

---

1. In the previous chapter, we learned that we have called methods directly without creating an instance for the respective class. However, this was only possible because we had defined the methods as `static`. We will come back to this later on.

Calling a method, for instance, the programmer expects that the method will process the current instance. If he calls output.vect1(), the programmer expects that the coordinates of the instance vect1 will be output. If the programmer calls add.vect1(vect2), he/she expects that the submitted vector vect2 is added to the instance vect1. If we want to add vect1 to vect2, we call vect2(vect1).

But, how does a method process the actual instance for which it is called? Very simple: by accessing the data elements of the method definition. Therefore, if we define the method output() in the class as follows:

```
void output()
   {
   System.out.println("(" + x + "," + y + ")");
   }
```

it means that we output the *x* and *y* coordinates of the instance that calls the method:

```
vector vect1, vect2;

vect1.x = 10;
vect1.y = 29;
vect2.x = -1;
vect2.y = 12;

vect1. distribute();       // output (10,29)
vect2.distribute();        // output (-1,12)
```

The implementation of the method addUp() is now easier to understand.

```
void add(vector v)
   {
   x += v.x;
   y += v.y;
   }
```

Here, the *x* and *y* coordinates of the vector object v are submitted to the coordinates of the actual instance (represented with x and y) and the result is saved in the coordinates of the actual instance. (Remember that the combined assignment x += v.x; will correspond to the assignment x = x + v.x;.)

The constructor

At the beginning of this chapter, we said that in the instance formation (of a variable of the type of a class) a specific method is always called, i.e. the *constructor*. The constructor always has the same name as the class. In the case of our vector, class `vector`, the constructor is therefore called `vector()`.

We have also learnt that the compiler creates an internal standard constructor for all classes in which no constructor is defined in the source text. However, this does not mean that you have to be satisfied with this standard constructor generated by the compiler, or that you have to leave the creation of the constructor to the compiler. On the contrary, it works both ways: the concept of class requires that each class has a constructor, and the compiler guarantees this also for classses where the constructor was forgotten by the programmer, or was left out. Why is the constructor so important for the class?

The constructor is called once for each instance created by a class – namely in the instance formation. This explains its purpose: it needs to guarantee that the instance is initialized correctly. The constructor is usually employed to assign the initial values to the data elements. You can also write in the constructor any other arbitrary statement that can be executed automatically in the instance formation.

If you define such constructors, take into account the following points:

• Constructors always have the same name as their classes.

- Constructors have no return value, and no return type (not even `void`) is given in the definition.

- Constructors are called automatically in the instance formation.

- Constructors cannot be called explicitly for an instance as other methods.

5 Set up a constructor for the `vector` class.

```java
// vector calculation
import java.lang.*;

public class vectorcalculation
    {
  public static void main(String[] args)
        {

        }
    }


class vector
    {
    // Instance variables
    double x;
    double y;

    // Constructor
    vector()
      {
      x = 0;
      y = 0;
      }

    // Methods
    void addUp(vector v)
      {
      x += v.x;
      y += v.y;
      }

    void distribute()
      {
      System.out.println("(" + x + "," + y + ")");
      }

    }
```

As required, our constructor is called like the class and was declared without return type. In the constructor, we assign the value 0 to the data elements x and y.

6 Create two instances of the vector class and assign them the values using the point operator. Now add the second vector to the first and distribute the first vector again.

```java
// vector calculation
import java.lang.*;

public class vectorcalculation
   {
  public static void main(String[] args)
      {
        vector v_1 = new vector();
        vector v_2 = new vector();

        v_1.x = 10;
        v_1.y = 30;

        v_2.x = 12.5;
        v_2.y = -1.5;

        v_1.addUp(v_2);
        v_1.distribute();
        }
   }

class vector
   {
   // Instance variables
   double x;
   double y;

  // Constructor
  vector()
     {
     x = 0;
     y = 0;
     }

   // Methods
   void addUp(vector v)
     {
     x += v.x;
     y += v.y;
     }

   void distribute()
      {
      System.out.println("(" + x + "," + y + ")");
      }
   }
```

7 Save the program as `vectorcalcuation.java`. Compile and execute it (Figure 12.4).

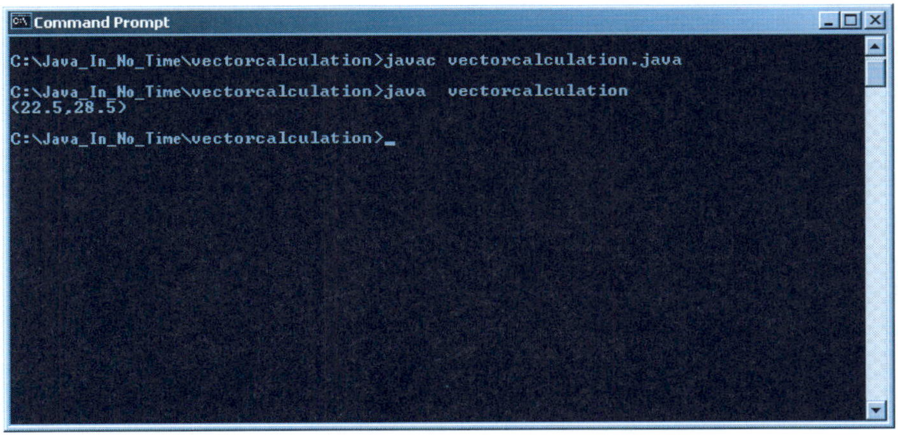

Figure 12.4: Output of the program vectorCalculation.

Arrays of objects

You already know how an array is created by the variables of a simple data type:

```
// an Array of  5 float variables
float[] field = new float[5];
```

When you create an array of objects, the situation is a bit more complex. The analogue definition is not sufficient:

```
vector[] field = new vector[5];
```

On the contrary, unlike simple variables, object variables do not contain any object, only a reference . Thereby the definition above has created just a field of references (that do not show anything and therefore have the value `zero1`), but no real objects yet. You have to finish it for each array entry using an explicit initializiation with `new`:

```
int i;
for(i = 0;  i < 5;  i++)
    {
    field[i] = new vector();
```

187

However, the access is carried out as usual on the point operator, e.g.:

```
System.out.println("field[4]: x = "+ field[4].x);
```

You will learn more about the references in the next chapter, where we explain how to use objects as parameters.

Chapter 13

More about classes

In this chapter, we continue our learning about classes.

Several constructors

If you have studied the vector program that we developed at the end of Chapter 12, you may have noticed that the constructor that is provided is quite useless. It initializes the coordinates to zero. We then have to assign the correct coordinates in explicit calls using the dot operator (e.g. v_1.x = 10). This not very elegant. It would be much more practical and simple if we could initialize these instance variables directly while creating the instances, and if the initialization were the primary benefit of a constructor.

This is possible. You can define several constructors as well as the default constructor. The only condition is that they must be different in the type and number of their parameters.

For this, we do not need to replace the old constructor vector(), but we can draft a second additional constructor that takes on two arguments, x_start and y_start, and assigns them the data elements x and y.

1 Begin a new program, vectorcalculation2.java, and take on the source text in vectorcalculation.java. Replace the previous class name vectorcalculation with vectorcalculation2.

2 Set up a second constructor for vector that takes on two double arguments to initialize the x and y coordinates.

```
// vector calculation2
import java.lang.*;

public class vectorcalculation2
    {
  public static void main(String[] args)
      {
      vector v_1 = new vector(10,30);
      vector v_2 = new vector(12.5, -1.5);

      v_1.addUp(v_2);
      v_1.distribute();
      }
    }

class vector
    {
    // instance variables
    double x;
    double y;

    // constructor
    vector()
      {
```

```
x = 0;
y = 0;
}

vector(double x_start, double y_start)
  {
  x = x_start;
  y = y_start;
  }


// Methods
void addUp(vector v)
  {
  x += v.x;
  y += v.y;
  }

void distribute()
  {
  System.out.println("(" + x + "," + y + ")");
  }
}
```

We have two constructors with the same name. It has to be like this because constructors always take on the name of their class. However, we have also learnt that the identifiers (names of the defined program elements) must be unambiguous, meaning there cannot be two elements with the same name, otherwise the compiler cannot distinguish between the elements. The same happens for constructors. Here, the compiler uses a trick. It internally appends the parameter list of methods (and also constructors that belong to them) in coded form to the method names. In doing so, it can distinguish between methods and constructors that have the same name, but different parameter lists (different parameter number or data types).

WHAT IS THIS?

Creating different methods of the same name that differ only in the parameter lists is described as an overload. In the call, the compiler recognises, by the arguments adopted, which of the overloaded methods needs to be called.

If our `vector` class has a constructor to draft initial values, we can run the instancing in `main()` in a much more elegant way. In the creation using `new`, we submit the desired values to the constructor and the additional setup using point notation can be avoided.

Access specification

During the course of this book, you have met access specificators (e.g. `public`) several times. Now it is time to deal with these tools.

Let's have a look at the clipping from the old vector program again, in which we have executed the initialization of the coordinates by means of accessing the dot operator:

```
vector v_1 = new vector();
vector v_2 = new vector();

v_1.x = 10;
v_1.y = 30;
v_2.x = 12.5;
v_2.y = -1.5;
```

What is actually happening here? At this point, we work outside of the instances `v_1` and `v_2` of the `vector` class and set its instance variables `x` and `y` to new values. According to the object-oriented theory, this is not right. Objects are independent, delimited units, and not everyone should be allowed to access the insides of the class.

For this reason, in each object-oriented programming language there is an *access specifier*, i.e. a special keyword that determines who can access the methods and variables of a class.

You can distinguish between two different kinds of access: access from inside and access from outside:

- Inside in this context means within the class definition, and access from inside means that you access other elements (data elements or other methods) of the same class from a method definition.

  So, for instance, the method `add up()` of the class `vector` accesses the data elements `x` and `y` from inside:

  ```
  void addUp(vector v)
      {
       x += v.x;
       y += v.y;
      }
  ```

- Outside in this context means out of the class definition and access from outside means that you access an instance to an element (data element or method) of the class.

  So, for example, we access the variables for the coordinates using the dot operator in the `main()` method of our program, as shown above.

Classes always allow access from inside. Things are different with access from outside. In this case, the creator of the class can establish the rights of access at definition time (which is also called visibility). Different steps are allowed:

- `public`: methods and instance variables marked like this are visible in the methods of the class itself, in the methods of the child[1] classes and from outside, i.e. all classes are accessible.

- `protected`: visible in the class itself and in the derived classes, as well as in the classes of the same package. Classes that are called from other packages cannot be accessed.

- `private`: only visible in the class itself. `private` variables stay concealed for derived classes and for the caller of instances.

- Methods/variables without an access specificator have standard visibility (*package scope*), i.e. they can only be called by classes (more precisely, in their methods) that belong to the same package.

Programmers who use a class in their program are not interested in the details of the class definition. They only require the functionality, and therefore suitable methods that enable them to access the class. Anyone who

---

1. Derived classes inherit features and methods from their basic class. This concept of inheritance is introduced in Chapter 14.

creates a new class usually makes sure that they strictly limit access by limiting the use of `private/protected` or package scope and only allowing certain points of access by means of `public`.

In doing so, the principle of *information hiding* is created. An external user of a class cannot freely operate on the data of the class and cause damage. They can only access what is harmless or protected by suitable access methods.

> **WHAT IS THIS?**
>
> *All public elements of a class are also defined as the public interface of the class.*

If you look at the information in `vectorcalculation2.java` again, you will see that all methods (except for `main()`) and variables have been defined without an access specificator, i.e. all have package scope: each class belonging to the same package can call them. None of the other classes can use them.

But how can you tell whether two classes belong to the same package? It is quite easy if the source code of this class (whether it is in the same file or in a different file) is given in the same directory.[2] For this reason, we can also access the elements of `vector` in the frame class `vectorcalculation2`, because both classes belong to the same package.

Let's now turn to the legendary `main()` method. It has been defined as `public`. This is mandatory regulation because you know that `main()` is a very special method. And because `main()` must only be called from outside (namely by the Java runtime), it has to be able to be called by anyone, i.e. `public`.

You may be wondering how the definition of `vectorcalculation2` fits into what has been said about the access specificator.

```
public class vectorcalculation2
    {
    // ....
    }
```

---

2. In the real world, the rules are a bit more extensive and complex, but this simple rule is enough for our purposes.

`public` (as single access specificator) can also stand in front of the keyword `class`. A class that is labelled in this way is visible to classes of other packages. However, this is not actually important within the framework of this book.

> **NOTE**
>
> *Each Java program needs a class defined as* `public` *because this will provide a method that is defined as* `public static void main(String[] args)`. *The source text file that contains this class must have the same name as this class (and the extension* `.java`, *of course).*

You should already know this from previous chapters. If you get ominous error messages during compilation, check that your program follows the above rules.

Now let's use our new knowledge about access specificators and scatter a few in the vector program. What could we improve?

Private data elements – public methods

A rule of thumb for a good class design is that you should declare data elements as `private`.

This means that, if necessary, you shield the variables of a class from the outside world. Nobody will be able to manipulate them freely. At this point, a small problem arises: what if you want not writing access but reading access to a particular variable from outside?

A declaration as `private` forbids both of these. The trick is to define special methods for access to private variables that are provided to the outside world as `public`. The programmer of the class can control what exactly can be done with the innards of the class using this method. You can have two different kinds of methods: those that provide the value of a private variable and those that set the value.

Now we will practice this in our vector program by making the coordinates `private` and providing the corresponding GET methods for reading access.

3 Declare the variables of the class `vector` as `private`.

```java
// vectorcalculation2
import java.lang.*;

public class vectorcalculation2
    {

  public static void main(String[] args)
      {
      vector v_1 = new vector(10,30);
      vector v_2 = new vector(12.5,-1.5);

      v_1.addUp(v_2);
      v_1.distribute();
      }
    }

class vector
    {

    // instance variables

    private double x;
    private double y;


    // constructor
    vector()
      {
      x = 0;
      y = 0;
      }

    vector(double x_start, double y_start)
      {
      x = x_start;
      y = y_start;
```

```
    }

  // Methods
  void addUp(vector v)
    {
    x += v.x;
    y += v.y;
    }

  void distribute()
    {
    System.out.println("(" + x + "," + y + ")");
    }
  double getX()
    {
    return x;
    }

  double getY()
    {
    return y;
    }
  }
```

Notice that the methods of the class `vector` can operate unhindered on x and y, since this is access from inside. This also works with different instances. In the case of the method `addup()`, we access x and y directly from another instance using the point notation from vector. This is allowed and therefore works.

4 Save the program as `vectorcalculation2.java`. Compile and execute it (Figure 13.1).

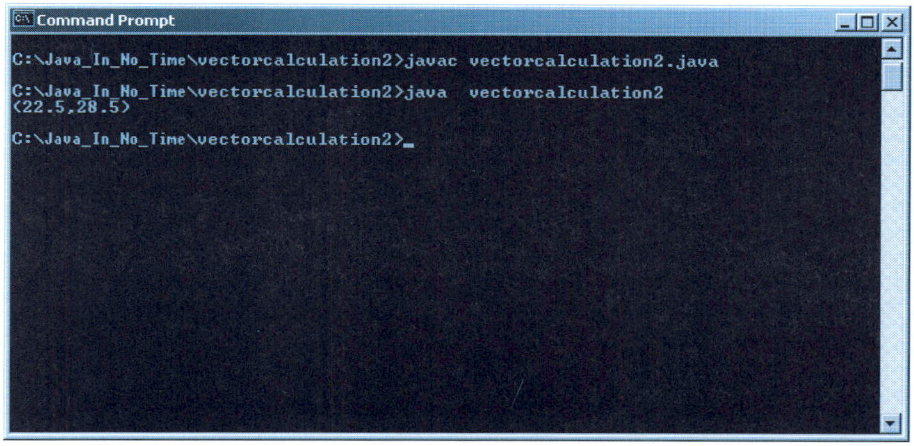

Figure 13.1: Output of the program vectorcalculation2.

The vector program

To conclude, we would like to point out that there is a more extensive implementation of the vector program in the accompanying CD in the subdirectory *vectorProgram* from Chapter 13, in which further methods (subtraction, scalar multiplication etc.) are implemented.

Objects as parameters for methods

Call by reference

In Chapter 10 we talked about methods and introduced an important concept, namely *call by value*. This means that the value of a variable submitted as parameter is copied in the parameter variable. The method that is called always operates on one copy only. An example:

```
class Example

  {
  void thenethod(int theParameter)
    {
    theparameter++;
    System.out.println("Value here:   " + the parameter);
    }
  }

// Call in the main() method
int a = 10;
example bsp = new example();
bsp.themethod(a);
System.out.println("Value in main is" + a);
```

Can you work out which output we should expect to see on the screen? In `main()` we call `themethod()` and submit the variable `a` with the actual value `10`. `themethod()` takes on the parameter and increases it by one. Consequently, the `println()` statement provides the value of 11 in the method. So far, no problems. Now the program jumps back to the call in `main()` and carries on with another `println()` output. The value of 10 is output again.

The reason for this is the call-by-value mechanism. The method has just one copy, and what it does with its copy has no consequences on the position that is called.

Now you can, of course, submit not only simple data types such as int, double etc. as parameters to methods, but also objects. However, here there is an important peculiarity that is connected to the nature of object variables. Let's consider a variable definition once more:

```
int a = 234;
vector b = new vector();

vector b;
b = new vector(30,20);
```

The case is clear in the variable a. A memory cell is reserved in the main memory and connected with the name a. We can begin straight away and save a number there. When creating an object, things are a bit more complicated. So far, we have only shown the variant vector b = new vector(30,20). However, this is just a simple notation, which the compiler allows. We will see what actually happens below: first of all, a variable b of the vector type is created. In the second step, a more suitable memory area is obtained by means of the new operator, and the address of this memory area is saved in the variable b. This kind of variable that does not contain a real value, but just a memory address, is called reference.

Therefore, object variables are references to the actual objects and do not contain them themselves (Figure 13.2).

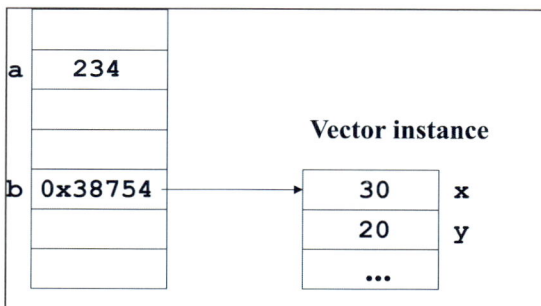

Figure 13.2: Object variables refer to the actual objects.

In our example, b only contains the address (here 0x38754) of the memory cell in the main memory where the object is located.

You may be wondering why you need to know this. Maybe it does not matter to the programmer where the data is saved internally. This is true. But sometimes this knowledge is necessary. An example of this is when submitting objects as parameters of methods.

Let's assume now that a vector is submitted to a method as a an argument:

```
void harmless(vector v)
    {
    v.x = 0;
    }
```

How does this assignment work? (For this example, we assume that access to x is not limited with `private` etc.) The methods operate on a copy of the submitted `vector` object, as arguments are always given as call by value. And now you have to be careful! We submit a copy of the object variable that only contains a memory address. During access using the dot operator, the Java compiler follows this address to the actual memory area of the object and works on the original ("original" is the wrong word in this context, because the object itself does not create a copy, only the reference does).

> **CAUTION**
>
> *Objects that are submitted to the methods as arguments are not submitted as a copy, but are submitted by the reference, i.e. the called method can operate on the original object. This process is also called call by reference.*

Arrays as parameters

You might be surprised that this topic appears in this chapter, because, so far you have not learnt that arrays are objects. For this reason, the `new` operator is used both in the definition of arrays and normal objects.

Programmers can remember very few object characters of an array. Above all, the instance variable `length` (we briefly mentioned this in chapter 11 regarding the size of an array) is worth mentioning:

- The definition as a parameter is similar to that of an array, e.g.

  ```
  void theMethod(int[] field)
      { ... }
  ```

The difference is that square brackets have to be placed after the data type in a definition. In this way, the compiler recognizes that an array has to be submitted. In the case of the call itself, only the array name is submitted, in the same way as any other object or simple data type:

```
int[] measurements = new int[100];

theMethod(measurements);
```

- Because an array is a disguised object, you will not be surprised if the submission as argument is also carried out as call by reference during the method call. This means that statements inside a method operate on the original, since no copy is created:

```
void theMethod(int[] field)
   {
   field[0] = 10;   // operates on the
                    // originalarray!
   }
```

To get more practice of working with arrays as parameters, we are going to expand the vector program to include a method that adds a vector to a given array.

1 Begin a new program, vectorcalculation3.java, and adopt the source text of vectorcalculation2.java. Replace the previous class name vectorcalculation2 with vectorcalculation3.

2 Add a new method ToArray() to the vector class, which contains an array of vector as a parameter.

```
// vectorcalculation3
import java.lang.*;

public class vectorcalculation3
   {
   public static void main(String[] args)
      {
      }
   }
class vector
   {
   // instance variables
   private double x;
   private double y;

   // constructor
   vector()
      {
      x = 0;
      y = 0;
      }
   vector(double x_start, double y_start)
      {
      x = x_start;
      y = y_start;
      }

   // Methods
   void add(vector v)
      {
```

```
  x += v.x;
  y += v.y;
  }
void distribute()
  {
  System.out.println("(" + x + "," + y + ")");
  }

double getX()
  {
  return x;
  }

double getY()
  {
  return y;
  }

void addToArray(vector[] v)
  {
  }
}
```

3 In the new method, the coordinates of the `vector` instance are added to all vectors in the submitted array.

```
void addToArray(vector[] v)
    {
    int i;
    for(i = 0; i < v.length; i++)
      {
      v[i].x += x;
      v[i].y += y;
      }
    }
```

4 Create an array in `main()` with five vectors and (1,1) as the coordinates and insert the method `addToArray()`.

```
public static void main(String[] args)
      {
      vector[] vectors= new vector[5];
      for(int i = 0; i < vectors.length; i++)
        {
        vectors[i] = new vector(1,1);
        }
      }
```

First of all, the variable `vectors` is defined as an array of the `vector` type with five entries. Unlike simple data types such as `int`, the actual objects are not yet created, as only enough space for the references (of the addresses) has been reserved because of the reference characters of the object variables. Therefore, you have to create an instance for each entry in a loop with the `new operator` and assign these to the array.

5 Create an instance of vector, which is added to the vectors of the array, using the method addToVector().

```java
public static void main(String[] args)
    {
    vector[] vectors = new vector[5];

    for(int i = 0; i < vectors.length; i++)
      {
      vectors[i] = new vector(1,1);
      }

    vector vec = new vector(10,20);
    vec.addToArray(vectors);

    for(int i = 0; i < vectors.length; i++)
      {
      System.out.println("vector " + i + " ("
                  + vectors[i].getX() + ", "
                  + vectors[i].getY() + ")");
      }
    }
```

The instance vec calls its method addToArray() and it adds itself to each vector of the submitted array.

6 Save the program as vectorcalculation3.java. Compile the program and execute it (Figure 13.3).

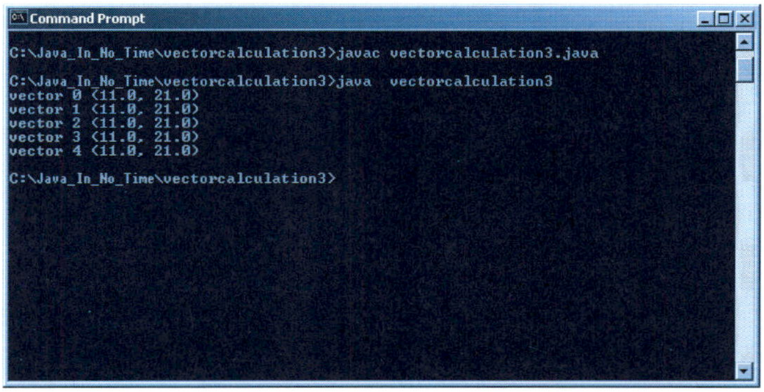

Figure 13.3: Output of the program vectorcalculation3.

203

Static methods

We now want to look at one final peculiarity connected to classes: *static methods*. We have already met these once in Chapter 10. There, we put the keyword `static` at the beginning of every method during their definition. In Chapters 12 and 13, we didn't need to use `static` (except for the obligatory `main()` method). In order to avoid confusion, we will explain it again:

1. Class methods can only be called if an instance is created by the affiliated class. A call using the class name is allowed. In the example of our `vector` class:

```
vector.distribute()            // not possible!!
vector v = new vector(10,20);
v.distribute()                 // so it is ok!
```

2. Sometimes, however, it is practical to call a method directly without creating any instance of the affiliated class. In this case, we would invent `static`. We can use it for both methods and variables, placing `static` in front of it in the definition:

```
static void distribute()
    {
    }
```

The call of a static method is carried out using the class name, e.g.

```
vector.distribute();
```

When using `static`, notice that a static method can only operate in variables that are also defined as `static`. For instance, if you define the method `distribute()` as static in the class `vector`, the compiler would complain, because within `output()` the variables x and y are accessed, but they only exist provided that another instance of `vector` also exists. In this case, the only remedy is to define the affiliated variables as `static`:

```
class vector
    {
    static double x;
    static double y;
    ....
    }
```

We also proceed in this way when we have to call other methods from a static method. In this case as well, only static methods can be called. This was why, in Chapter 10, all methods were made as `static`. Because the `main()` method is always `static`, all the other methods also have to be static, because in that chapter, classes and instances were not yet available. In the meantime, you are now able to define and instance classes.

A prominent example of static methods is the class `Math`. It provides several mathematical methods (we have already learnt `Math.sqrt()`, for example) that were defined as `static` and can be called directly on the class names. Therefore, you do not need to create a separate instance for the class `Math`.

Summary

In object-oriented programming, beginners must deal with a large amount of new, unfamiliar ways of thinking. You have already met several important (but not all) concepts and rules, some of which we still have to go into more detail. However, in order to maintain a general overview, we will now list the most important points again:

- Classes are (self-defined) data types.

- Variables of class types are defined as instances. The values of these instances are the objects of the class.

- In the class definition, you can establish which data elements the objects of the class have, and which methods need to be used to process objects.

- The instancing of a class has two parts. First a corresponding instance variable (i.e. `vector instancevariable;`) is created. Then an object is created by means of the `new` operator and is assigned to the instance variables. As long as no object is assigned, an instance variable has the value zero.

- During the instancing of an object of the class (also called instance formation), a special method of the class, which we call a constructor, is automatically called. We can define separate constructors in the class in order to assign initial values to the data elements of the objects, during instance formation.

- The constructor has the same name as the class and has no return value. Several constructors with various parameter lists are possible.

- Basically, all of the elements of a class have package behaviour, meaning that all classes belonging to the same package can access the methods and variables of the class.

- Access to methods and elements is carried out by means of the dot operator (`class name.method()`).

- In order to program in a controlled way with the instances of a class, as little as possible should be visible to the outside world, by making all elements `private`. For controlled exchange with the outside world, public (package scope or `public`) GET/SET methods are available.

- Objects are submitted not as a copy but as a reference. Alterations are effective on the original thanks to a method. This is also the case for arrays, which are also objects in essence.

- By inserting the keyword `static`, methods are defined as static and can be called directly using the class name without an instance.

Chapter 14

Inheritance

You have now learnt a lot about Java. You know that it is object-oriented and therefore sees the world as a set of objects in which features and activities are combined as variables and methods. The second pillar of object orientation is inheritance, which we will learn in this chapter by looking at its essential features.

The basic idea

Try to imagine that you need to write a Java program to help a personnel department manage a company's employees. At this point, as an object-oriented thinker, you will soon hit on the idea of defining classes or objects for this purpose. It should occur to you to define a class called employees and define suitable features and activities for it. Typical features are, for instance:

- name, first name
- address
- position
- salary

For the sake of simplicity, we will consider just one of the possible activities (i.e. methods), `increase salary()`.

We set a corresponding class definition:

```
class Employees
   {
   // features
   String name;
   String first_name;
   String position;
   int    salary;

   // constructor
   Employees(String name,  String first_name,
             String position,  int salary)
      {
      name       = name;
      first_name  = first_name;
      position = position;
      salary    = salary;
      }
   }
```

After that, we would also need the method for salary increase that contains a percentage and raises the current salary. Finally, we need a method to output the data:

```
class Employees
   {
   // features
   String name;
   String first_name;
   String position;
   double salary;
```

```
// Methods
Employees(String name, String first_name,
                    String position, double salary)
  {
  name = name;
  first_name  = first_name;
  position = position;
  salary  = salary;
  }

void increasesalary(double p)
  {
  salary = salary * (1 + p/100.0);
  }

void distribute()
  {
  System.out.println("name      : " + first_name +
                       " " +name);
  System.out.println("position : " + position);
  System.out.println("salary    : " + salary+
                       " EUR");
  System.out.println();
  }
}
```

So far, so good. Now you could directly create a Java program that uses this class concretely, and that creates an instance of employees for each employee and, for example, manages all instances in a large array:

```
Employees[] personnel = new Employees[100];
personnel[0] = new Employees("Watkinson","Paul",
                "Production Manager",18000);
personnel[1] = new Employees("Burton","Jon",
                            "Web Designer",15000);
personnel[2] = new Employees("Mitton","Jonathan",
                            "IT Manager", 16000);
// etc.
```

If, at the end of the year, salaries have to be raised by five per cent (let's assume that the company's business is doing well!) you could elegantly run through the array in a loop through and call the method `increase salary()` for each employee:

```
int i;
for(i = 0; i < 100; ++i)
  {
  personnel[i].increasesalary(5.0);
  }
```

Let's assume that management has decided to increase the software developers' salary. The employees who have this position are given 1.5 times the normal increase, for instance 7.5 per cent in five per cent. How is this

209

converted in the Java project above? A way out would be to install an `if` query to increase the salary in the loop:

```
int i;
for(i = 0; i < 100; ++i)
   {
   if((personnel[i].Position).equals("Production Manager")
      personnel[i].increasesalary(7.5);
   else
   personnel[i].increasesalary(5.0);
   }
```

However, this is untidy and expensive. Apart from this, the source text becomes difficult to read. Before, it was easy to see what was being done; now you have to look more carefully.

Another option would be to transfer this `if` inquiry to the method `increase salary()`. This would be much better as the readability of the Java program would be guaranteed. However, imagine that the class `Employees` provides more methods then in our mini example (e.g. for the administration of the holiday quota, travelling expenses, daily allowance, etc.) that have to distinguish which position the respective instance of `Employees` has. It is easier to imagine that the source text would be swarming with `if` or `switch`. And imagine the chaos if something had to be changed afterwards. Innumerable places have to be searched and changed in the source text. Something is obviously bound to go wrong in this case.

Therefore the best solution is inheritance. This idea is to build a hierarchy of classes. First, we find a general base class from which special versions are derived. The base class has properties and methods that are valid for all classes from this hierarchy. The derived classes extend the functionality of the base class with respect to its needs.

So far so good. But what happens now? Let's go back to our example. In case of inheritance, we would proceed as follows: the class `Employees` is defined as a base class, as we did previously. From this, we derive an instantiation, e.g. software developer. We then adapt the method `increase salary()` in this class (therefore add the factor 1.5), and that's all we need to do. The main loop in `main()` can remain unchanged. Now let's see how this is done.

Creating derived classes

It is better to begin at the front and carry on step by step in the same manner.

1 Create a new program, `inheritancedemo.java`, and begin with the basic framework.

```
// inheritance
public class inheritancedemo
   {
   public static void main(String[] args)
      {
      }
   }
```

2 Create the base class `Employees` as shown above.

```
// inheritance
public class inheritancedemo
   {
   public static void main(String[] args)
      {
      }
   }

class Employees
   {
   // features
   String name;
   String first_name;
   String position;
   double salary;

   // Methods
   Employees(String Name, String First_name,
                 String Position, double Salary)
      {
      name       = Name;
      first_name  = First_name;
      position = Position;
      salary     = Salary;
      }
   void increasesalary(double p)
      {
      salary = salary * (1 + p/100.0);
      }

   void distribute()
      {
      System.out.println("name      : " + first_name +
                        " " +Name);
```

```java
        System.out.println("position : " + position);
        System.out.println("salary   : " + salary +
                        " EUR");
        System.out.println();
        }
    }
```

3 Then create a class Software Developer from Employees.

```java
// inheritance
public class inheritancedemo
    {
    public static void main(String[] args)
        {
        }
    }

class Employees
    {
    // features
    String name;
    String first_name;
    String position;
    double salary;

    // Methods
    Employees()
        {
        }

    Employees(String Name, String First_name,
                    String Position, double Salary)
        {
        name       = Name;
        first_name  = First_name;
        position = Position;
        salary   = Salary;
        }

    void increasesalary(double p)
        {
        salary = salary * (1 + p/100.0);
        }

    void distribute()
        {
        System.out.println("Name     : " + First_name + " "
                                        + Name);
        System.out.println("Position : " + Position);
        System.out.println("salary   : " + salary + " EUR");
        System.out.println();
        }
    }
```

```
class ProductionManager extends Employees
   {
   }
```

The definition of a derived class is, in principle, carried out in the same way as any other normal class definition; however, the keyword `extends` followed by the name of the base class is added after the class name. Furthermore, in any case a base class needs a default constructor. For this reason, we have to add the class `Employees` (even if it does not actually carry on).

The new class `Software Developer` has now automatically inherited all features and methods from its base class `Employees` (apart from what was protected by the access specificator; see Chapter 13).

However, we have to consider the constructor for `Software Developer`. The constructors of `Employees` themselves cannot be inherited continually. However, the Java compiler of course requires a constructor called `SoftwareDeveloper()` when instancing `Software Developer`. Therefore:

4 Add the necessary constructors to the derived class.

```
// inheritance
public class inheritancedemo
   {
   public static void main(String[] args)
      {
      }
   }


class Employees
   {
   // features
   String name;
   String first_name;
   String position;
   double salary;

   // Methods
   Employees()
      {
      }

   Employees(String Name, String First_name,
                        String Position, double Salary)
      {
      name       = Name;
      first_name  = First_name;
      position = Position;
      salary     = Salary;
```

```
      }

   void increasesalary(double p)
      {
      salary = salary * (1 + p/100.0);
      }

   void distribute()
      {
      System.out.println("name      : " + first_name + " "
                                           + name);
      System.out.println("position : " + position);
      System.out.println("salary    : " + salary + " EUR");
      System.out.println();
      }
   }

class ProductionManager extends Employees
   {
   ProductionManager(String name, String first_name,
                   String position, double salary)
      {
      super(name,first_name,position,salary);
      }
}
```

Because the derived class does not have an additional variable, we can simply call the constructor of the base class. This is possible using `super()`. `super()` calls the constructor of the base class that expects the same parameter.

5 Add the instantiation for the derived class.

```
// inheritance
public class inheritancedemo
   {
   public static void main(String[] args)
      {
      }
   }


class Employees
   {
   // features
   String name;
   String first_name;
   String position;
   double salary;

   // Methods
   Employees()
      {
```

```
    }

  Employees(String Name, String First_name,
                    String Position, double Salary)
    {
    name       = Name;
    first_name  = First_name;
    position = Position;
    salary     = Salary;
    }

  void increasesalary(double p)
    {
    salary = salary + salary * (1 + p/100.0);
    }

  void distribute()
    {
    System.out.println("name       :" + first_name + " "
+name);
    System.out.println("position : " + position);
    System.out.println("salary    : " + salary + " EUR");
    System.out.println();
    }
  }

class ProductionManager extends Employees
  {
  ProductionManager(String name, String first_name,
                    String position, double salary)
    {
    super(name,first_name,position,salary);
    }

  void increasesalary(double p)
    {
    p *= 1.5;
    salary = salary * (1 + p/100.0);
    }
  }
```

We create an identical method `increase salary()`: the same name, the same parameter, the same return type. We only modify the method part by increasing the submitted percentage by half. The method of the base class is overtyped with the definition of this method.

6 Create some employees in an array in the `main()` method and execute a salary increase.

```
// inheritance
public class inheritancedemo
  {
  public static void main(String[] args)
```

```
      {
      Employees[] personal = new Employees[3];

      personal[0] = new ProductionManager("Watkinson",
                        "Paul",
                        "Production Manager",180000);
      personal[1] = new Employees("Burton","Jon",
                        "Web Designer",150000);
      personal[2] = new Employees("Mitton",
                        "Jonathan",
                        "IT Manager", 160000);

      for(int i = 0;  i < 3;  ++i)
        {
        personal[i].increasesalary(5.0);
        }

      for(int i = 0;  i < 3;  ++i)
        {
        personal[i].distribute();
        }

      }
   }
class Employees
   {
   // features
   String name;
   String first_name;
   String position;
   double salary;

   // Methods
   Employees()
      {
      }

   Employees(String Name, String First_name,
                          String Position, double Salary)
      {
      name=Name;
      first_name  = First_name;
      position = Position;
      salary    = Salary;
      }

   void increasesalary(double p)
      {
      salary = salary * (1 + p/100.0);
      }

   void distribute()
```

```
    {
    System.out.println("name      : " + first_name + " "
                       +name);
    System.out.println("position : " + position);
    System.out.println("salary   : " + salary + " EUR");
    System.out.println();
    }
}


class ProductionManager extends Employees
  {
  ProductionManager(String name, String first_name,
                    String position, double salary)
    {
    super(name,first_name,position,salary);
    }

  void increasesalary(double p)
    {
    p *= 1.5;
    salary = salary * (1 + p/100.0);
    }
  }
```

To begin with, we create a small array of the Employees type, i.e. the type of the base class. When instancing objects and assigning to the single array entries, we can use objects of both the base class Employees and Software Developer. This is really practical. When running through the array for the salary increase we always call the method increase salary, but depending on the actual class type, we call either the method of the base class or the method of the derived class with the modified calculation. The Java runtime environment itself does this automatically.

7 Save the program as inheritancedemo.java. Compile and execute it (Figure 14.1).

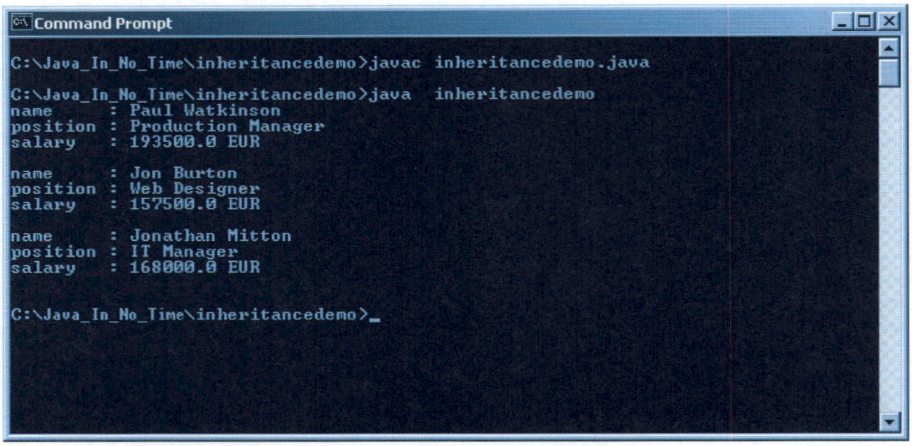

Figure 14.1: Output of the Demo program for inheritance.

```
Command Prompt                                               _ □ ×

C:\Java_In_No_Time\inheritancedemo>javac inheritancedemo.java

C:\Java_In_No_Time\inheritancedemo>java   inheritancedemo
name      : Paul Watkinson
position  : Production Manager
salary    : 193500.0 EUR

name      : Jon Burton
position  : Web Designer
salary    : 157500.0 EUR

name      : Jonathan Mitton
position  : IT Manager
salary    : 168000.0 EUR


C:\Java_In_No_Time\inheritancedemo>_
```

Chapter 15

Programming with files

After the difficult chapters about object-oriented programming, we have earned ourselves some relaxation. Programming with files is certainly not the easiest of themes, but it is not particularly difficult either.

Streams

In Java, any input and output, whether from the keyboard or the screen, in a file, or from and to any other conceivable device, is based on the concept of streams (Figure 15.1).

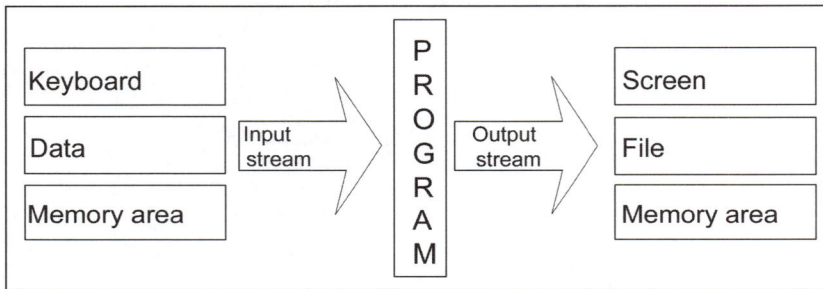

Figure 15.1: The stream model.

If we now wish to read data from a file on the hard disk, the file forms the source for the data stream. The reverse of this is that the file is the destination of the data stream while writing.

Writing in files

Writing in files is carried out in four steps:

1. Integration of the Java package `java.io`.

2. Creation of the stream object that is connected to the file.

3. Writing in the file.

4. Closing the output stream to the file.

It certainly sounds complicated! Most points are implemented quickly and simply – you just have to know how.

1 Create a new program, `FileOutput.java`, and begin with the following basic framework:

```
// Write in the files
import java.io.*;

public class FileOutput
   {
   public static void main(String[] args)
                                  throws IOException
     {
     }
   }
```

Note that in the definition of a method that executes the stream-based inputs/outputs, you need to report to the compiler that a non-recoverable error has occurred. This is possible by means of `throws IOException`.

2 Create an instance of the class `FileWriter`. This instance is our output stream and creates the combination with the file.

```
// Write in files
import java.io.*;

public class FileOutput
   {
   public static void main(String[] args)
                                  throws IOException
     {
     FileWriter fileStream =
                    new FileWriter("test.txt");
     }
   }
```

The constructor of `FileWriter` contains the required file name as argument. In the instruction of a file name in a Java program, you also need to pay attention to something else:

In addition to this, you should notice that in the procedure shown above, a file that is already available is replaced with the same name without any warning, therefore it is overtyped.

3 Create an instance of the class `PrintWriter` that contains the output stream as argument.

```java
// Write in files
import java.io.*;

public class FileOutput
  {
  public static void main(String[] args)
                              throws IOException
    {
    FileWriter fileStream = new FileWriter("test.txt");

    PrintWriter output =
                  new PrintWriter(fileStream);
    }
  }
```

The `PrintWriter` class possesses some methods for an easier output of the text, in particular (the already known) `print()` and `println()` methods, which are used in the same way as the methods of `System.out`, which have the same name.

4 Write the data in the file.

```java
// Write in files
import java.io.*;

public class FileOutput
  {
  public static void main(String[] args)
                            throws IOException
    {
    FileWriter fileStream = new FileWriter("test.txt");
    PrintWriter output = new PrintWriter(fileStream);
    // Write
    // different data to test in the file
    String text1 = "This is a text";
    int    var1  =  1000;
    String text2 = "This is another text";
    double var2  =  555.111;

    output.println(text1);
    output.println(var1);
    output.println(text2);
    output.println(var2);
    }
  }
```

5 Close the output stream.

```java
// Write in files
import java.io.*;

public class FileOutput
  {
  public static void main(String[] args)
                            throws IOException
    {
    FileWriter fileStream = new FileWriter("test.txt");
    PrintWriter output = new PrintWriter(fileStream);
    // Write
    // different data to test in the file
    String text1 = "This is a text";
    int    var1  =  1000;
    String text2 = "This is another text";
    double var2  =  555.111;

    output.println(text1);
    output.println(var1);
    output.println(text2);
    output.println(var2);

    output.close();

    }
  }
```

If you no longer require an output stream, you should close it by calling the `close()` method of the stream. This is why the file is opened and can also access other programs. In the previous `println()` instructions, the data submitted are buffered in the main memory for the first time. In fact, the data are written on the hard disk in the required file first during the transmission of a certain amount of data or the call of `close()`. In other words, if the computer or the program crashes before the `close()` method is executed, the data could still be in the main memory and are therefore lost.

6 Save the program as `FileOutput.java`. Compile and execute it (Figures 15.2 and 15.3):

Figure 15.2: Execution of the file output program.

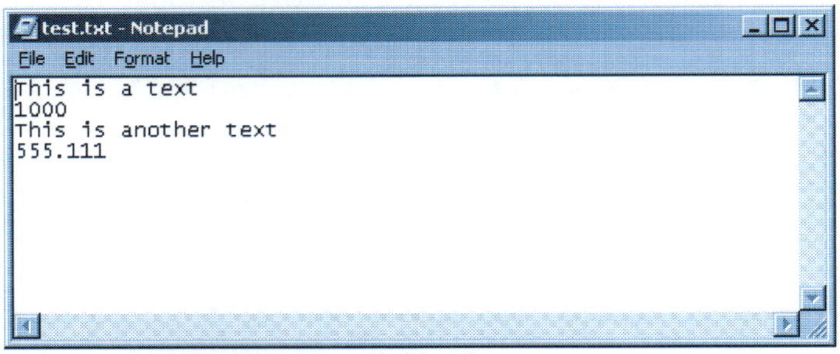

Figure 15.3: The data generated by the program.

Reading from files

Reading from files is quite similar to writing files:

1. Integrate the Java packet `java.io`.

2. Create the stream object that is connected to the file.

3. Read from the file.

4. Close the input stream to the file.

Usually, it is problematic to read data from the file.

1 Create a new program, `FileInput.java`, and begin with the following basic framework:

```
// Read from files
import java.io.*;

public class FileInput
  {
  public static void main(String[] args)
                            throws IOException
    {
    }
  }
```

2 Create an instance of the class `FileReader`. This instance is our input stream and establishes the connection with the file.

```
// Read from files
import java.io.*;

public class FileInput
  {
  public static void main(String[] args)
                            throws IOException
    {
    FileReader fileStream = new FileReader(
                    "FileInput.java");
    }
  }
```

The class `FileReader` represents the exact counterpart of `FileWriter`. Its constructor expects a string together with the file that has to be read.

3 Create an instance of `BufferedReader` that is connected with the input stream. This class has the method `readLine()` to read the text in lines more easily.

```java
// Read from files
import java.io.*;

public class FileInput
   {
   public static void main(String[] args)
                                   throws IOException
     {
     FileReader fileStream = new FileReader(
                                 "FileInput.java");

     BufferedReader input =
                 new BufferedReader(fileStream);
     }
   }
```

4 The actual reading is carried out in a loop by means of `readLine()`.

```java
// Read from files
import java.io.*;

public class FileInput
   {
   public static void main(String[] args)
                                   throws IOException
     {
     FileReader fileStream = new FileReader(
                                 "FileInput.java");

     BufferedReader input =
                       new BufferedReader(fileStream);

     String line;

     while(true)
       {
       line = input.readLine();

       if(line == null)
         break;

       System.out.println("Fed: " + line);
       }
     }
   }
```

The method `readLine()` always reads a complete line and returns it as a string. If the return value is `zero`, then the end of the file is reached and we exit the endless loop with `break`.

5 Close the input stream.

```
// Read from files
import java.io.*;

public class FileInput
  {
  public static void main(String[] args)
                                throws IOException
    {
    FileReader fileStream = new FileReader(
                                  "FileInput.java");

    BufferedReader input =
                      new BufferedReader(fileStream);

    String line;

    while(true)
      {
      line = input.readLine();

      if(line == null)
        break;

      System.out.println("Fed: " + line);
      }

    input.close();
    }
  }
```

6 Save the program as FileInput.java. Compile and execute it (Figure 15.4).

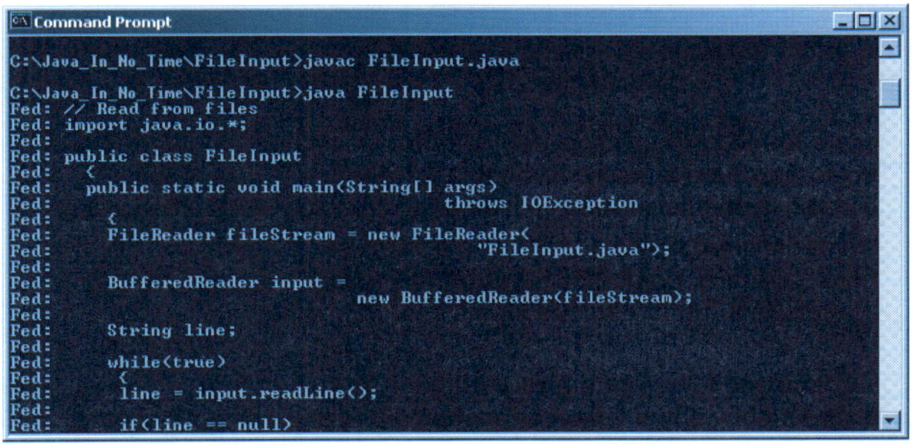

Figure 15.4: Reading the content of a Java source text, and outputting it on the console.

The capital city quiz

In the next and final chapter we will look at a few more techniques and then you will be a fully-fledged Java programmer. Before you put the book down, we want to create a larger and more complex program: your very own masterpiece!

The program is a quiz program that queries the capital cities of different countries.

The concept

To support the program, we will create a database as a simple text file. In this database we save the country/capital city combinations, which the program will query later.

The process of operations of the program will look like this:

- The program opens the database and determines how many data records (each country/capital combination corresponds to a data record) are saved in the file.

- Then the program selects one of the data records from the database (the selection should be random) and reads the country and capital.

- Finally, the program asks the user for the capital of the country, reads the input from the user, checks whether the right capital was input, and outputs the answer.

You will meet some new issues here, in particular how to create random numbers and how the data read by a file can be processed.

The implementation

1 Create a new program, `Quiz.java`, and begin with the basic framework:

```java
// Quiz of capitals
import java.io.*;

public class Quiz
    {
    public static void main(String[] args)
                                    throws IOException
        {
        }
    }
```

2 Create the database of the program.

Using an editor such as Notepad create a simple text file and save it under the name `Quiz.txt` in the directory of the program.

First type in the number of the data records and then the country/capital combinations.

```
9
Angola Luanda
Colombia Bogota
USA Washington
Switzerland Bern
Sweden Stockholm
England London
France Paris
Germany Berlin
Japan Tokyo
```

If you read data from a file in a program, you usually have to follow the format of the data of the file when setting the input routine. Since we are creating the file to read ourselves, we are in the lucky position to order the data in any way we want.

We begin the database with a line that only contains the total number of data records (also called *records*). After that, come the names of the countries in lines followed by the capital. Using this ordered setup we make the reading easier in the following.

3 Open a data base file.

```
// quiz of capitals
import java.io.*;

public class Quiz
  {
  public static void main(String[] args)
                             throws IOException
    {
    FileReader fileStream = new FileReader("Quiz.txt");
    BufferedReader input = new BufferedReader(fileStream);
    }
  }
```

You are already familiar with these instructions. The instance of `FileReader` produces the input stream of the data base file. The `Buffered Reader` class is created to facilitate the use of `readLine()` method.

4 Read the number of the data records saved in the file.

```
// quiz of capitals
import java.io.*;

public class Quiz
```

```
      {
   public static void main(String[] args)
                              throws IOException
      {
      FileReader fileStream = new FileReader("Quiz.txt");

      BufferedReader input =
                    new BufferedReader(fileStream);

      // Read number of entries
      String line;
      int number;

      line = input.readLine();
      number = Integer.parseInt(line);
      }
   }
```

The number of data records is the first instruction in the file. As usual, we read the first line and convert the available number contained there as character string into an integer that we assign to the variable number.

5 Select a data record.

```
// quiz of capitals
import java.io.*;
import java.util.*;

public class Quiz
   {
   public static void main(String[] args)
                              throws IOException
      {
      FileReader fileStream = new FileReader("Quiz.txt");

      BufferedReader input =
                    new BufferedReader(fileStream);

      // Read the number of entries
      String line;
      int number;

      line = input.readLine();
      number = Integer.parseInt(line);

      // A random number between 1 and number
      Random chance = new Random();
      int random_number;

      while(true)
         {
         random number = random.nextInt(number+1);
```

```
        if(random_number != 0)
           break; // number is ok
        }
     }
  }
```

It would be really boring if the program asked for the same capital in each call, so we will create the program so that it selects a random data record.

For this purpose, we take a random number between 1 and the total number of the data records. If the program takes, for instance, 3, this means that the capital of the country has to be queried from the third data record.

To create a random number in the `java.util` package we use the class `Random`, from which we generate an instance. It provides the method `next Int(n)`, which creates a random number between 0 and *n* (exclusive). For this reason, we submit `nextInt()` as an argument `number+1`, so that the last entry of the database can also be selected. The other way round, 0 is not a valid value for us, so 0 is not accepted and another number is asked for. For this reason, we insert the `while` loop, which will run until a random number that is not equal to 0 is created.

You may be wondering how a computer creates random numbers. A computer always executes only certain statement strings (programs). They are highly deterministic. In fact, a computer cannot actually create a random number sequence. It works according to a determined algorithm and generates a number whenever `nextInt()` is called. In doing so, a number sequence arises that appears to be random and irregular.

The algorithm that is used, according to its construction, predetermines the complete number sequence that can be created. The sequence recurs after a specific quantity of numbers. When creating a `Random` instance, it is established at what position in the number sequence the algorithm enters according to the number sequence of the algorithm. In doing so, we make sure that the same sequence of random numbers is not created when each program is run.

6 Read the country and the capital of the selected data record from the file.

```
// quiz of capitals
import java.io.*;
import java.util.*;

public class Quiz
   {
   public static void main(String[] args)
                                throws IOException
      {
```

```
FileReader fileStream = new FileReader("Quiz.txt");

BufferedReader input =
                      new BufferedReader(fileStream);

//Read number of entries
String line;
int number;

line = input.readLine();
number = Integer.parseInt(line);

// A random number between 1 and number
Random chance = new Random();
int random_number;

while(true)
   {
   random number = chancenextInt(number+1);
   if(random_number != 0)
      break; // number is ok
   }
// feed the line checked
for(int i = 1; i <= random_number; i++)
   line = input.readLine();
}
}
```

The number given indicates how many lines are to be skipped. Therefore we read the lines one at a time, and in the process overwrite the previous line if necessary. If the loop stops, the last line read from the file stands in the variable `line`.

Next, we have to solve this problem: in `line` there are two concepts that we have to split between two `string` variables, `country` and `capital`.

7 At this point, we need to solve this problem: in `line` there are two concepts we have to split under two `string` variables, `country` and `capital`.

```
//  quiz of caitals
import java.io.*;
import java.util.*;

public class Quiz
   {
   public static void main(String[] args)
                                       throws IOException
      {
      FileReader fileStream = new FileReader("Quiz.txt");

      BufferedReader input =
                      new BufferedReader(fileStream);
```

```
      // Read number of entries
      String line;
      int number;

      line = input.readLine();
      number = Integer.parseInt(line);

      //A random number between 1 and number
      Random chance = new Random();
      int random_number;

      while(true)
        {
        random_number = chance.nextInt(number+1);
        if(random_number != 0)
           break; // number is ok
        }

      // feed the checked line
      for(int i = 1; i <= random_number; i++)
         line = input.readLine();
      // extract country and capital
      StringTokenizer st = new StringTokenizer(line);
      String land = st.nextToken();
      String capital = st.nextToken();
      }
  }
```

Luckily, in the package `java.util` there is the suitable class for this aim – `StringToken`. We derive an instance from this and submit the character string that has to be parsed to the constructor. Calling the method `nextToken()` we get the individual words (= Tokens) one at a time from the character string.

8 Ask the user the capital of the selected country and evaluate their answer. After that, the input stream is closed.

```
// quiz of capitals
import java.io.*;
import java.util.*;

public class Quiz
  {
  public static void main(String[] args)
                                    throws IOException
    {
    FileReader fileStream = new FileReader("Quiz.txt");

    BufferedReader inputfile =
                    new BufferedReader(fileStream);

    // read number of entries
```

```
String line;
int number;

line = inputfile.readLine();
number = Integer.parseInt(line);

// A random number between 1 and number
Random chance = new Random();
int random_number;

while(true)
   {
   random_number = chance.nextInt(number+1);
   if(random number != 0)
      break; // number is ok
   }

//feed the line checked
for(int i = 1; i <= random_number; i++)
   line = inputfile.readLine();

// extract country and capital
StringTokenizer st = new StringTokenizer(line);
String country = st.nextToken();
String capital_city = st.nextToken();

System.out.print("Capital city of " + country + ": ");

BufferedReader keyboard =
    new BufferedReader(
            new InputStreamReader(System.in));
String answer = keyboard.readLine();

if(answer.equals(capital))
   System.out.println("The answer is correct!");
else
   System.out.println("Incorrect. Correct answer is" +
capital_city);

inputfile.close();
   }
}
```

9 Save the program as Quiz.java. Compile and execute it (Figure 15.5).

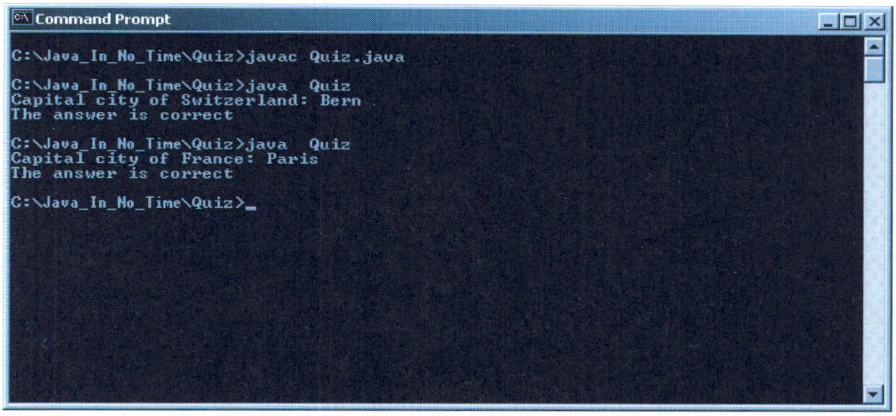

Figure 15.5: The Quiz *program.*

You can improve the program further by extending the database (do not forget to adapt the instruction of the grand total in the data record in the first line of the file). Another interesting extension would be to execute the inquiry of capitals within a loop (without having to start the program again every time).

Chapter 16

Conclusion and outlook

Now that you have become familiar with Java, its syntax and the creation of console applications, we want to look at some secondary techniques of Java programming. This is a brief overview rather than a detailed explanation. This chapter should increase your interest in Java and suggest other topics that you might wish to learn.

To begin with, we will show you how to create applets to support Web pages, and how to generate a simple graphical interface. After that, we introduce the Java debugger, with which you can track down logical errors in the programs. We will conclude the chapter with some tips and references for further development.

Applets

Applets are a true Java peculiarity. With Java, you can create not only programs for users, but also programs for Web pages. In this section you will learn how to achieve this task and which options are available for you.[1]

Imagine that you want to create a Web page whose topic is "diet and health". The visitors to your Web site should be able to have their body mass index calculated. However, it is impossible to achieve this by means of HTML code alone.

Certainly you can draft a text that describes how to calculate the body mass index and how the different index values have to be assessed. But this is not as attractive as a Web page with entry fields in which the visitor can enter their height and weight directly, and then press a button in order to calculate their body mass index (see Figure 16.1).

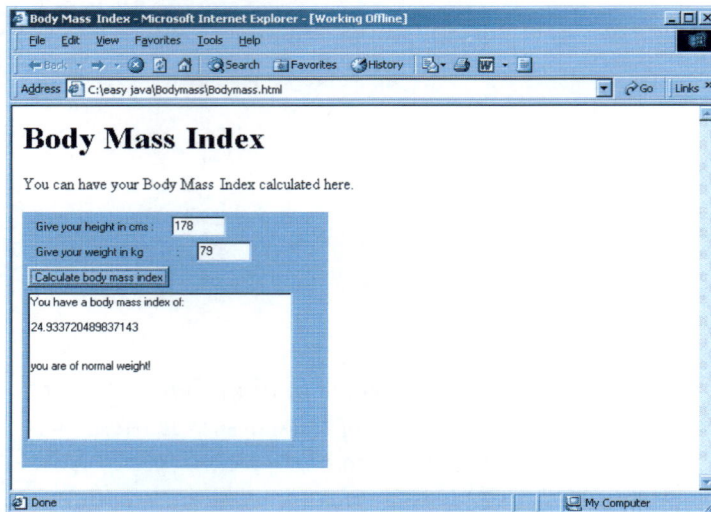

Figure 16.1: Web page with integrated applet.

You can create this kind of interactive Web page using Java.

---

1. We start with the assumptions that you use an Internet provider and that you are familiar with the creation and publication of Web pages.

JavaScript and CG

Java applets are not the only option for creating interactive, program-supported Web pages. Other options include creating a Java Script and using a CGI program.

JavaScript has little to do with Java: they simply share the name and an essentially similar syntax. JavaScript was developed specifically for Web page programming: the code can be written directly in the HTML code of the Web page, and you can react to mouse moves and other events in the Web page, as well as manipulate the individual HTML elements in the Web page (for instance, select a different background colour or shift an embedded picture). The latter operation is not possible with Java. However, Java is by far the most powerful programming language, and offers techniques and possibilities for advanced Web programmers that are not available in JavaScript. Moreover, Java applets are not downloaded as JavaScript programs as source text but as binary byte codes (.class file). To conclude, applets can normally be reused more easily than the JavaScript code.

CGI programs are programs that cannot be downloaded with the Web page on the Web visitor's computer. They are executed on the Web server. This has the advantage that – if the corresponding access rights have been set – from this kind of program you can access other server-sided stored files (for instance, a data base or another HTML file). CGI programs are normally used for the server-sided evaluation of form inputs (visitors' book, on-line orders etc.)[2]. They are not suitable on the pages of the Web visitor – in this case you should use JavaScript or Java.

---

2. This is not necessary in a simple program such as the calculation of body mass indices. A Web designer who is familiar with JavaScript would probably implement the calculation with JavaScript. However, this is not a valid argument against creating an applet.

Applets on the Web

Let's look at an applet from its creation in the programmer's editor to its execution in the browser of a Web surfer.

1. To begin with, write the source text of the applet and save it as a text file with the extension `.java`, as usual.

2. Call the Java compiler and submit the source text file to it. If the source text contains no errors, the compiler generates a byte code file with the extension `.class`.

3. Now, create the Web page. Using the HTML tag `<applet>` applet is embedded in the Web page.

   We indicate the name and the location of the applet in the HTML tag. In the simplest case, we copy the `.class` file of the applet directly in the directory where the Web page in which the applet is called is.

At this point, let's change the subject and look at a Web surfer who has just made the Web page with the applet (Figure 16.2).

4. The browser loads the Web page, i.e. it sends a corresponding requirement to the Web server in which the Web site has been saved. The Web server sends it to it, together with the HTML code of the Web page and the `class` file of the applet.

5. The browser accepts the Web page and applet.

6. In order to execute the applet, the browser calls its integrated Java interpreter. It starts the applet.

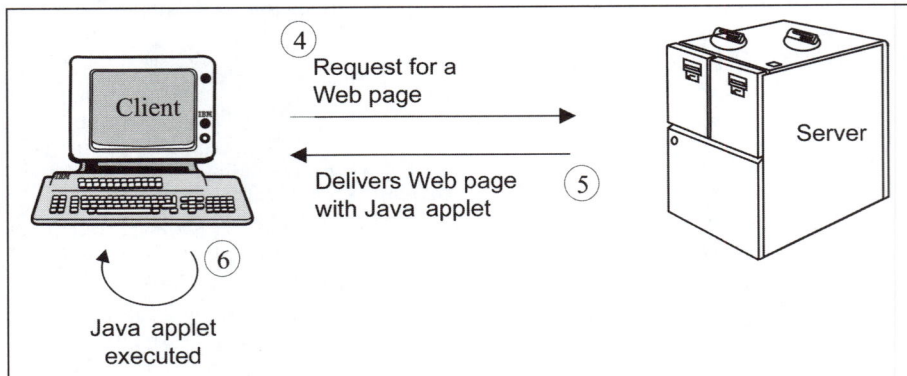

Figure 16.2: The execution of applets.

A first applet

Applets have their own basic framework. We will look at the structure in the example of a simple applet that gives the greeting "Hello World Wide Web".

1 Begin a new file, `HelloWWW.java`.

2 Import the required classes. For applets we need the classes `java.awt.Graphics` and `java.applet.Applet` at least.

```
// This is the first applet
import java.awt.Graphics;
import java.applet.Applet;
...
```

Here you can see that an import application is also only possible for one class. Alternatively, you can also import the complete package (e.g. `import java.awt.*;`).

3 Create the basic framework for the main class of the applet.

We name our first applet `HelloWWW`.

```
// This is the first applet
import java.awt.Graphics;
import java.applet.Applet;
public class HelloWWW
   {
   }
```

4 Derive the main class the applet from the class `Applet`.

```
// This is the first applet
import java.awt.Graphics;
import java.applet.Applet;

public class HelloWWW extends Applet
  {
  }
```

As you already know, Java provides many classes in the Java libraries. For example, there is the class `Applet`, which contains a number of methods that are important for applet programming: `paint()`, `init()`, `start()`, `stop()` and `destroy()`. In order to use these methods for our applet class `HelloWWW`, we give `Applet` as base class for our applet class `HelloWWW`.

```
public class HelloWWW extends Applet
```

You already know the keyword `extends` from Chapter 14. It informs the compiler that our class `HelloWWW` has to take on (inherit) all elements of the given base class (Applet).

The applet methods

Even if it does not look anything like that, our class `HelloWWW` now contains – derived from the class `Applet` – five methods called `paint()`, `init()`, `start()`, `stop()` and `destroy()`. This is good, because if the browser executes the applet, it calls these methods:

- `init()` is called if the browser loads the applet.

- `start()` is called if the browser starts the applet.

- `paint()`is called if the browser requires that the applet draws itself.

- `stop()` is called if the browser stops the applet (for example, because the user has left the page and has changed to another Web page)

- `destroy()`is called if the applet has been completely removed from the working memory.

Now our applet is able to work, but it is not doing anything yet. In order to activate it, we overwrite the methods inherited from the base class `Applet` (in this section we just overwrite the `paint()` method over).

5 Overwrite the `paint()` method.

```
// This is the first applet
import java.awt.Graphics;
import java.applet.Applet;
```

```
public class HelloWWW extends Applet
    {
    public void paint(Graphics gc)
        {
        }
    }
```

The peculiarity of applets is the fact that their output does not appear on the console but on the Web page where the applet has been embedded. As we will see in the next section, the browser reserves a special area especially for this purpose on the Web page, in which the output of the applet is embedded. This area is like a screen. However, on this screen you cannot write as you can on a console, but you can "draw" on it. We draft the drawing operations in the `paint()` method inherited from `Applet` that we overwrite for this purpose.

WHAT IS THIS?

To overwrite a method means to adopt the signature of an inherited method (name, parameter, return value) and to newly define it in a derived class.

The `paint()` method that we have inherited from the base class has the following signature:

```
void paint(java.awt.Graphics gc)
```

In order to overwrite the method in the `HelloWWW` class we define it in the class with the same signature
:

```
public class HelloWWW extends Applet
    {
    public void paint(Graphics gc)
        {
        }
    }
```

NOTE

We can write `Graphics` *instead of* `java.awt.Graphics` *when overwriting because we have imported* `java.awt.Graphics`.

6 Output the greeting 2Hello World Wide Web" in the `paint()` method.

```
// This is the first applet
import java.awt.Graphics;
```

243

```
import java.applet.Applet;

public class HelloWWW extends Applet
  {
  public void paint(Graphics gc)
    {
    gc.drawString("Hello World Wide Web!",100,50);
    }
  }
```

With your call, the `paint()` method creates an object of the class `java.awt.Graphics` and saves it in the parameter `gc`. But who calls the method `paint()`?

As we already know from the previous section, the method is called automatically by the browser if it decides that the applet has to be drawn again (which is practically always the case, when the browser has to rebuild the Web page with the applet – for example, when the user has temporarily covered up the browser with a different program and later brought it into the foreground again).

Before calling the `paint()` method, the browser creates an object of the type of the class `java.awt.Graphics`, which represents the part of the Web page that takes on the applet. This object submits the parameter `gc` during the call.

Now the parameter `gc` represents the canvas of the applet. However, it is also an object of the class `Graphics`, which defines a variety of character methods (Table 16.1).

Graphics method	Description

`clearRect(int x,`
`        int y,`
`        int width`
`        int height)`
	Fills the rectangle with a background colour from its top left corner (x, y), and its width and height.

`drawArc(int, int,`
`        int, int,`
`        int, int)`
	Draws an arch.

`drawLine(int x1,`
`        int y1,`
`        int x2,`
`        int y2)`
	Draws a line between the points (x1, y1) and (x2, y2).

`drawOval(int x,`
`        int y,`
`        int width,`
`        int height)`
	Draws an oval.
	The parameter defines a rectangle (given by means of the left corner above x,y as well as width and height) in which the oval is drawn.
	If width and height are equal, a circle arises.

Graphics method	Description

`drawPolygon(`
`    int[] xPoints,`
`    int[] yPoints,`
`    int numPoints)`
	Draws a polygon out of `numpoints` lines. The points between which lines are made are defined by means of the array `xpoints` and `ypoints`. The last line goes from the last to the first point.

`drawRect(int x,`
`    int y,`
`    int width,`
`    int height)`
	Draws a rectangle.
	
	The parameters define the top left corner x,y as well as the width and height of the rectangle.
	
	If width and height are equal we get a square.

`drawRoundRect(int x,`
`    int y,`
`    int width,`
`    int height)`
`    int archW,`
`    int archH)`
	Draws a rectangle with rounded corners.
	
	The parameters `archW` and `archH` indicate the horizontal and vertical diameters of the rounded corners.

`drawString(String str,`
`    int x,`
`    int y)`
	Gives a string of specific coordinates.

`fillOval(), fillPoly-` `gon(), fillRect() ...`	A series of methods to draw full forms (cf. `draw...()`).
`Color getColor()`	Returns the current drawing colour.
`Font getFont()`	Returns the current type used.

`setColor(Color)`	Defines the colours to use when drawing.
	
	You can submit one of the constants predefined in the Java libraries as a colour (`Color.black`, `Color.blue`, `Color.cyan`, `Color.darkGray`, `Color.gray`, `Color.green`, `Color.lightGray`, `Color.magenta`, `Color.orange`, `Color.pink`, `Color.red`, `Color.white`, `Color.yellow`):
	
	`gc.setColor(Color.green);`
	
	Or you can create a colour using the instruction of the colour quota for red, green and blue. Each colour quota can take on a value between 0 and 255.
	
	`// Set color on red`
	`gc.setColor( new Color(255, 0, 0) );`

245

Graphics method	Description

`setFont(Font)`	Defines the type to be used.
	
	We submit the type as a font object:
	
	`gc.setFont(`
	`        new Font("TimesRoman",`
	`            Font.BOLD | Font.ITALIC,`
	`            24) );`
	
	We submit the name of the type (or one of the predefined logic font names) to the `Font` constructor : `Dialogue`, `DialogueInput`, `Monospaced`, `Serif`, `SansSerif` and `Symbol`), the style (`Font.BOLD`, `Font.ITALIC` or `Font.BOLD | Font.ITALIC`) and the type size.

Table 16.1: A selection of some methods of the Graphics class.

By calling these character methods for the `gc` object we draw on the canvas of the applet.

In our example, we want to draw a text in the applet. For this purpose, we can use the method `gc.drawString()` that contains the character string "Hello World Wide Web!" that has to be drawn as parameter as well as the `x` and `y` coordinated of the place where the text will be displayed.

```
gc.drawString("Hello World Wide Web!",100,50);
```

7 Save the applet as `HelloWWW.java` and compile it with `javac` in the usual way.

In order to execute and test the applet, we now need another suitable Web page that integrates the applet.

Integrating applets into Web pages

We create a simple Web page to test the applet, which apart from the applet has no other content than a short text.

1 Create a new file in your text editor.

2 Type in the basic framework of the HTML page.

```
<!DOCTYPE html PUBLIC "-//W3C//DTD HTML 4.01//EN"
  "http://www.w3.org/TR/html4/strict.dtd">

<html>
```

```
<head>
  <title> </title>

</head>

<body>

</body>

</html>
```

3 Indicate a title for the Web page and insert a short text that will be displayed in the Web browser.

```
<!DOCTYPE html PUBLIC "-//W3C//DTD HTML 4.01//EN"
    "http://www.w3.org/TR/html4/strict.dtd">

<html>

<head>
  <title>First Applet</title>

</head>

<body>

<p>Web page calls Applet. Please answer.</p>

</body>

</html>
```

4 Integrate the applet into the Web page.

```
<!DOCTYPE html PUBLIC "-//W3C//DTD HTML 4.01//EN"
    "http://www.w3.org/TR/html4/strict.dtd">

<html>

<head>
  <title>First Applet</title>

</head>

<body>

<p>Web page calls Applet. Please answer.</p>

<applet code="HelloWWW.class"
        width="300"
        height="100">
</applet>
```

```
</body>
```

```
</html>
```

To embed the applet, the `<applet>` tag is used.
Three attributes are set in the `<applet>` tag:

- `Code`: the name of the applet file (optional with `.class` extension).

- `Width`: the width of the area (in pixels) that the applet takes on in the Web page.

- `Height`: the height of the area (in pixels) that the applet takes on in the Web page.

If the applet is not located in the same directory as the HTML document, you also have to set the `codebase` attribute and indicate in it the absolute or relative path to the applet file. If the HTML file is located in the directory `c:\easy java\HelloWWW.html` for example, and the applet code in the directory `c:\easy java\HelloWWW` the code base is set as follows:

```
<applet code="HelloWWW.class"
        codebase="../applets"
        width="100"
        height="80">
```

```
</applet>
```

> **NOTE**
>
> *In this case, we have used the `<applet>` tag for embedding the applet. At present, this is common practice, even if the `<applet>` tag is considered as obsolete and should no longer be used. Instead, the standard recommends the `<object>` tag. The embedding of applets with the `<object>` tag (see below) is currently only supported by the Netscape 6 Browser. Therefore, at the moment, you are still encouraged to give preference to the `<applet>` tag.*
>
> ```
> <p>
>  <object
>         codetype="application/java"
>         classid="java:HelloWWW.class"
>          width="300" height="100">
>
> Sorry,  your  browser  does  not  support  any  Java
> applet.</object>
>  </p>
> ```

5 Save the Web page under any name with the extension `.html` or `.htm` in the same directory as the Java applet (we have called the HTML file after the applet `HelloWWW.html`).

6 Load the HTML file in your browser (Figure 16.3).

The prerequisite is that the applet is displayed correctly in the browser and the browser is Java-capable (therefore has a suitable Java interpreter integrated that is not too old) and is configured so that applets are started and executed.

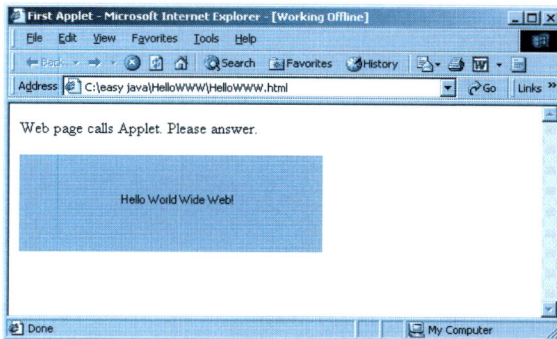

Figure 16.3: Web page with an applet in the browser.

NOTE

If you do not have a browser, you can also test the applet in the appletviewer of the JDK. Call the console (in Windows this is the MSDOS prompt) and change to the directory with the HTML file. Call the appletviewer and submit the HTML file to it:

```
PROMPT> appletviewer HelloWWW.html
```

Java programs with graphical user interfaces

We talk about a graphical user interface (GUI) if a program has a window that appears when we call the program, and has menu bars, tool bars, control elements (such as buttons, list, and input or option buttons), dialogues, scroll bars, working areas, etc.). For many users, the window (with its different decorations) is identical to the program because the window appears automatically when we call the program, and when we close the window, the program is also exited.[3] For programmers, the windows and dialogues of a program do not represent the actual program, but the user interface of the program. By means of the user interface, the user can control the program, send input to the program, and see the output of the program.

A partial description of all the possibilities for the styling of GUIs with Java would be well beyond the scope of this book. Therefore, we will focus on a limited section: the use of control elements and the construction of a simple input mask.

Programming with control elements

WHAT IS THIS?

Control elements are small, predefined interface elements that have a particular functionality. You will be familiar with most control elements, such as buttons, entry fields, option fields and scroll bars, from working with computers.

The integration of a control element into the user interface of a program is executed in five steps:

1 Define a variable for the control element.

```
Button myButton;
```

Indicate one of the control element classes predefined in Java – in our case `Button`. Apart from `Button`, in the Java libraries, a complete series of classes for control elements is also defined. Table 16.2 lists the most important of these.

---

3. In addition to this, few Windows users are familiar with the console and the execution of console programs.

Class	Control element
`Button`	Button
`Label`	Label (static text field)
`Text field`	Single-line text and entry field
`Text area`	Multi-line text and entry field
`Check box`	Option field
`List`	List field

Table 16.2: The most important Java AWT control element classes.

All the control element classes above are defined in the package `java.awt`, which is why we also talk about AWT control elements.

> **NOTE**
>
> *In addition to the AWT control element classes, there is a second set of control element classes – the swing control elements. The swing control elements are more powerful and modern, so we suggest that you use them. However, the swing control elements have been available since version 1.2 of Java. Many Web surfers are still using browsers that work with older Java interpreters that do not support the swing yet. For this reason, we use the AWT classes here.*

2 Create and open the control element.

To create the control element, call the constructor of the control element class. Depending on the control element, you can submit one or more arguments to the constructor to configure the control element.

So, in the example above, we create a new `Button` object using the keyword `new` and a new `Button` constructor. The `Button` object is assigned to the variable `myButton` with which we can access the button later during the course of the program.

The title of the button can be submitted to the `Button` constructor as a `String` argument. The size of the button is adapted to the width of the title automatically.

3 Place the control element on the user interface of the program.

```
setLayout(new FlowLayout());
add(myButton);
```

To include a control element in an applet, call the `add()` method of the applet and submit the control element to it.

To order the control elements, Java uses *layout managers* (Table 16.3). These are instances of predefined classes that take on the ordering of elements for you.

In the example above, we created a `FlowLayout` manager and set it up using the method `setLayout()` as a layout manager of the applet. The `FlowLayout` manager puts the control elements into the applet in the order in which they are inserted by means of `add()`, onto the screen of the applet from left to right. If a control element does not fit onto the current line any more, the layout manager begins a new line.

Constructor	Order	Addition of components by means of:
`FlowLayout()`	One after the other	Add(components)
`BorderLayout()`	According to five fields: Central, North, East, South, West	Add("East",Components) Add("Center",Components) etc.
`GridLayout(n,m)`	In grid format in *n* x *m* Matrix	In lines: Add(Components1-1) Add(Components1-2) Add(Components1-3) etc.

Table 16.3: A selection of the most simple layout managers.

NOTE

The order of the control elements using layout managers is not so simple. The advantage of the layout managers is that they allow you to insert the interface elements relatively easily and without having to indicate explicit coordinates. Moreover, they adapt the order of the elements according to the size of the display area (the applet area in the Web page or the window of an application). Things become more complex when you want to control the order of elements directly. In this case, you should encapsulate the layout managers in each other and/or use more complex layout managers, such as Grid BagLayout.

4 Set up the code that will be executed if the user works in a particular way with the control element.

```
class eavesdropper implements ActionListener
  {
  public void actionPerformed(ActionEvents)
    {
    // Code that is executed, when the event
    // has entered
    }
  }
...
myButton.addActionListener(new eavesdropper());
```

Now things become really complex. Let's focus on the basic principle.

How can the user work with this control element? They can click on it, move the mouse over it, or press a button while the control element is activated. There are predefined methods for all of these events that you can implement and connect to the control element.

> **WHAT IS THIS?**
>
> *An interface is like a class in which we can only define methods without any statements. If you want to use a method from an interface, derive your own class from the interface using the keyword* implements *and define the methods of the interface in this class.*

For instance, to intercept the clicking of a button, we normally use the method `actionPerformed()`, which is implemented in the interface `ActionListener`.

If you therefore want a variable `demo` to be set to 3 each time a button is pressed, define a new class (such as `eavesdropper`) that is derived from the interface `ActionListener` and implements the method `actionPerformed()` so that in the method the value of the variable `demo` is set to 3.

```
class eavesdropper implements ActionListener
  {
  public void actionPerformed(ActionEvents)
    {
    demo = 3;
    }
  }
```

After the class for the event treatment is set, you have to connect it with the control element. Once again, there are special methods predefined in the classes of the control elements. Buttons (objects of the class `Button`) have the method `addActionListener()`, for example. Then you have just to call this method for the button and submit an object of the previously defined event class to it.

```
myButton.addActionListener(new eavesdropper());
```

> **NOTE**
>
> *The line*
>
> ```
> myButton.addActionListener(new eavesdropper());
> ```
>
> *is an abbreviation for*
>
> ```
> eavesdropperObject = new eavesdropper();
> myButton.addActionListener(eavesdropperObject);
> ```

5 Access the new control element to query or modify its status.

By "status" of a control element, we mean a particular control element with specific features whose value we can query or set from the program.

For a `Label` control element you can, for instance, query or set the text in the label again using the methods `getText()` and `setText()`. The same methods are also defined for the `TextField` and `TextArea` control elements and are used to query the text input in the control element or to display a new text in the control element.

```
TextField input;

input = new TextField(10);   // entry field, the 10
                             // Characters is extended
...
String str;
str = input.getText();       // Save text from entry field in
                             // String str
```

Input masks for applets

Now that we have become familiar with the fundamental steps of programming with control elements, we want to look at a rather more complex example: how to create an input mask for applets using control elements.

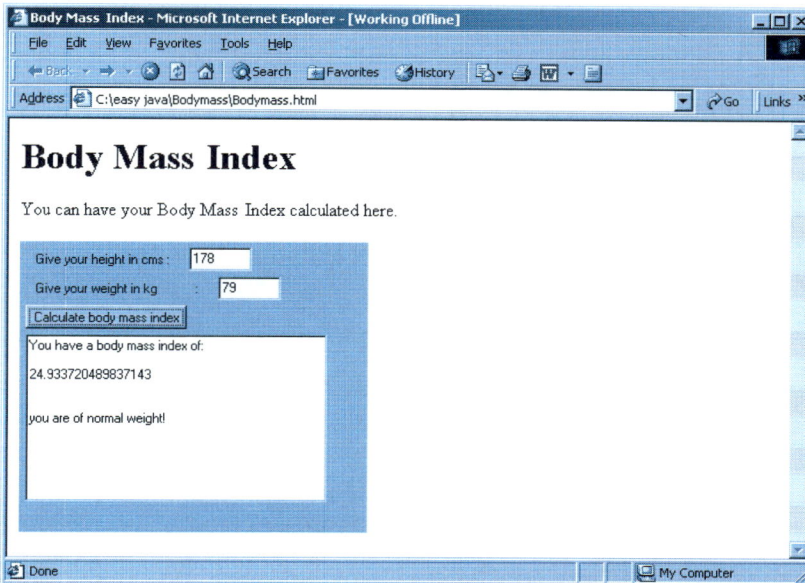

Figure 16.4: The body mass applet.

The applet described in the following is used to calculate the body mass index. It uses two `TextField` control elements to read height and weight details as well as a `TextArea` control element to output the result. For the calculation to be executed, the reader of the Web site should input the height and weight and then press the button (see Figure 16.4).

```
// Body Mass Applet
import java.awt.*;
import java.awt.event.*;
import java.applet.*;

public class BodyMass extends Applet
  {
  Label      l_height, l_weight;
  TextField t_height, t_weight;
  Send button     b_;
  TextArea  t_output;
  class eavesdropper implements ActionListener
    {
    public void actionPerformed(ActionEvents)
      {
      String title;
      String tmp;
      double height, weight, index;
      title = e.getActionCommand();

      if (title.equals("calculate Body Mass Index "))
```

```
            {
            tmp = t_height.getText();
            height = Double.valueOf(tmp).doubleValue();
            tmp = t_weight.getText();
            weight = Double.valueOf(tmp).doubleValue();

            index = weight/(height/100*height/100);

            t_output.setText(
                "You have a Body Mass Index of:\n\n");

            t_output.append(String.valueOf(index));

            if(index < 20)
              t_output.append(
                  "\n\n\nYou are under-weight!");
              else if (index >= 25)
                  t_output.append(
                      "\n\n\nYou are over-weight!");
              else
                  t_output.append(
                      "\n\n\nYour weight is normal!");
            }
        }
    }

public void init()
    {
    l_height = new Label
            ¬("Indicate your height in cm:");
    t_height = new TextField(5);

    l_weight = new Label
          ¬("Indicate your weight in kg             :");
    t_weight = new TextField(5);

    b_send = new Button("calculate Body Mass Index");

    t_output = new TextArea(10, 40);

    setLayout(new FlowLayout(FlowLayout.LEFT));

    add(l_height);
    add(t_height);
    add(l_weight);
    add(t_weight);
    add(b_send);
    add(t_output);

    b_send.addActionListener(new eavesdropper());
    }
}
```

After the usual `import` statements, the definition of the applet class `Body Mass` begins, and the variables for the control elements are declared first:

```
public class BodyMass extends Applet
  {
  Label      l_height, l_weight;
  TextField t_height, t_weight;
  Button     b_send;
  TextArea   t_output;
  ...
```

To be able to distinguish between the variable names, we have inserted a prefix at the beginning that points out which kind of control element we are dealing with.

This is followed by the definition of the `eavesdropper` class, which we can define directly in the class of the applet:

```
...
  class eavesdropper implements ActionListener
    {
    public void actionPerformed(ActionEvents)
      {
      String title;
      String tmp;
      double height, weight, index;

      title = e.getActionCommand();

      if (title.equals("calculate Body Mass Index"))

        {
        tmp = t_height.getText();
        height = Double.valueOf(tmp).doubleValue();
        tmp = t_weight.getText();
        weight = Double.valueOf(tmp).doubleValue();

        index = weight/(height/100*height/100);

        t_output.setText(
            "You have a  Body Mass Index of:\n\n");

        t_output.append(String.valueOf(index));

        if(index < 20)
          t_output.append(
                  "\n\n\nYou are under-weight!");

          else if (index >= 25)
             t_output.append(
                  "\n\n\nYou are over-weight!");

          else
             t_output.append(
```

```
                    "\n\n\nYou have a normal weight!");
        }
      }
    }
...
```

In the `actionPerformed()` method, it is determined which button the event has come from. The command name of the control element activated (which is equal, by default, to the title of the control element) is saved in the parameter e and can be called by means of the `getActionCommand()`. If this title is the same as that of our button (if the condition `if(title.equals("calculate Body Mass Index"))` is fulfilled), the calculation of the body mass index begins.

First, the height and weight inputs are queried by the `TextField` control elements and are converted into `double values`. We can calculate the Index value from these values. The result is output along with an explanatory text in the `TextArea` control element (in which the method `setText()` overwrites the old text in the control element while the method `append()` appends further strings to the current text).

Beneath the `eavesdropper` class comes the method `init()`. As you may remember, `init()` belongs to the applet methods that are inherited by the base class and are automatically called by the browser. The method `init()` is called if the browser loads the applet. We use it to set up the control elements.

First, we create the control elements:

```
. . .
 public void init()
   {
   l_height = new Label
          ¬("  Indicate your height in cm :");
   t_height = new TextField(5);

   l_weight = new Label
        ¬("  Indicate your weight in kg          :");
   t_weight = new TextField(5);

   b_send = new Button("Calculate the body mass index ");

   t_output = new TextArea(10, 40);
. . .
```

Then the layout manager is defined. Here, we use the `Flow Layout` manager, whose constructor we submit the constant `FlowLayout.LEFT` to so that the control elements in every new line are left aligned.

```
. . .
   setLayout(new FlowLayout(FlowLayout.LEFT));
. . .
```

Then we insert the control elements in the applet:

```
. . .
   add(l_height);
   add(t_height);
   add(l_weight);
   add(t_weight);
   add(b_send);
   add(t_output);
. . .
```

Finally, we connect the event method to the button:

```
. . .
   b_send.addActionListener(new eavesdropper());
   }
. . .
```

and exit the definition of the `Applet` class:

```
. . .
  }
```

As you can see, the large part of the applet code consists of the applications used for the creation of the GUI. The actual functional code of the applet is combined in the `actionPerformed()` method.

Input masks for GUI applications

Now that we have learned how to create GUIs, we need to learn how to write GUI applications correctly.

The following example shows how to create a GUI program for the calculation of body mass index (Figure 16.5).

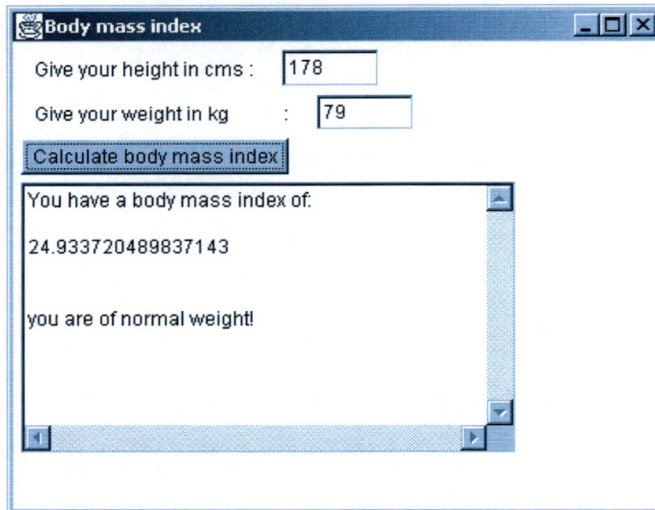

Figure 16.5: Window of the BodyMassGUI *application.*

```
// Body Mass GUI program
import java.awt.*;
import java.awt.event.*;


public class BodymassGUI extends Frame
    {
    Label      l_height, l_weight;
    TextField  t_height, t_weight;
    Button     b_send;
    TextArea   t_output;
```

```
class MyWindoweavesdropper extends WindowAdapter
   {
  public void windowClosing(WindowEvent e)
      {
      System.exit(0);
      }
   }

class eavesdropper implements ActionListener
   {
  public void actionPerformed(ActionEvent)
      {
     String title;
     String tmp;
     double height, weight, index;

     title = e.getActionCommand();

     if (title.equals("Calculate body mass index"))
        {
        tmp = t_height.getText();
        height = Double.parseDouble(tmp);
        tmp = t_weight.getText();
        weight = Double.parseDouble(tmp);

        index = weight/(height/100*height/100);

        t_output.setText(
            "You have a body mass index of:\n\n");

        t_output.append(String.valueOf(index));

        if(index < 20)

           t_output.append(
               "\n\n\nYou are under-weight!");

           else if (index >= 25)
              t_output.append(
                  "\n\n\nYou are over weight! ");

           else
              t_output.append(
                  "\n\n\nYou have normal weight!");
        }
     }
   }

BodymassGUI(String title)
   {
  super(title);

  l_height = new Label
          ¬("  Indicate your height in cm :");
```

261

```
        t_height = new TextField(5);

        l_weight = new Label
            ¬("  Indicate your weight in kg              :");

        t_weight = new TextField(5);

        b_submit = new Button("Calculate body mass index ");

        t_output = new TextArea(10, 40);

        setLayout(new FlowLayout(FlowLayout.LEFT));

        add(l_height);
        add(t_height);
        add(l_weight);
        add(t_weight);
        add(b_send);
        add(t_output);

        b_send.addActionListener(new eavesdropper());

        addWindowListener(new MyWindoweavesdropper());
        }

   public static void main(String[] args)

        {
        BodymassGUI window =
                new BodymassGUI("Body mass index");
        window.pack();
        window.setSize(400, 320);
        window.show();
        }
}
```

Let's look at what has changed in comparison with the applet version.

First of all, the `import` statement for the applet class has been discontinued and now the main class is called `BodyMassGUI`. However, it is more important that the main class is now derived from the Java class `Frame`. Thereby, our class becomes a window and the program becomes a GUI program.

```
...
public class BodymassGUI extends Frame
   {
   ...
```

The second important alteration follows: a second `eavesdropper` class is defined.

```
...
```

```
class MyWindoweavesdropper extends WindowAdapter
   {
   public void windowClosing(WindowEvent e)
      {
      System.exit(0);
      }
   }
...
```

The windows derived from `Frame` automatically has a framework and button to minimise, maximise or close. Nevertheless, the button to close the window is not connected with the functional code. Therefore, we have to establish what is going to happen when the window close button is pressed. Because this is the main window of the application, we want the application to be exited when the user presses the close button. To achieve this, we derive our own `eavesdropper class` from the `WindowAdapter` class and overwrite the method `windowClosing()`. In the method, we call the method `System.exit()`, which exits the current program.

WHAT IS THIS?

Adapter classes are special auxiliary classes that simplify the use of interfaces with several methods.

Later, in the constructor of the class, the `eavesdropper` class is connected to the main window of the application.

`addWindowListener(new MyWindoweavesdropper());`

The constructor of the `BodyMassGUI` class replaces the `init()` method of the applet. We define the constructor so that it adopts a title for the window. Using the predefined `method super()`, we pass this title on to the basis class `Frame`, which makes sure that the title is displayed in the title bar of the window...

```
BodyMassGUI(String title)
   {
   super(title);
   ...
```

After this, we set up the control elements and the connection of the button and the window (of the `BodyMassGUI` object itself) with their event treatment methods.

```
   ...
   b_send.addActionListener(new eavesdropper());
   addWindowListener(new MyWindoweavesdropper());
   }
```

The last alterations concern the `main()` function of the application.

```
...
  public static void main(String[] args)
    {
    BodyMassGUI window =
            new BodymassGUI("Body mass index");
    window.pack();
    window.setSize(400, 320);
    window.show();
    }
}
```

This begins with the creation of the window, i.e. an object of the class `BodyMassGUI`. The following method calls order the control elements in the window, determine the size of the window and display the window on the screen.

Debugging programs

The programmer's work of compiling and linking the application is very rarely complete. After that comes the testing of the program, combined with the eradication of errors (bugs).

> **NOTE**
>
> *The term "bug" was coined at Harvard University, where a moth penetrated the circuit board of the computer.*

Bases

If the compiler converts the source code of your program without any error message and an executable program file is created, you know that the source code is syntactically correct. However, this does not mean that the program is already doing what it was created to do.

- A minus sign may have been inserted into a formula where a plus sign should have been.

- The 21st element of an array may be accessed when the array was only created for 20 elements.

- The user may input a negative number where the program expects a positive number (and the program refrains from checking the correctness of the input – see the example of the calculation of the root).

It could be quite difficult to eliminate such errors in larger programs. Therefore there are special programs that help you with the fault diagnosis. This program is described as a *debugger*.

> **WHAT IS THIS?**
>
> *A debugger is a program that can execute another program step by step. Provided special debug information is available in the debugged program (identifiers and line numbers used in the program etc.), during the execution of the debugged program, the debugger can show which source text line is being executed, and which actual values are saved in the variables of the program.*

In practice, a session with a debugger is structured so that you always have to repeat the following three steps:

1. Execute the program in the debugger.

2. Stop the program at the point that you notice something is wrong and suspect an error.

3. Test the content of the variables to find out where the error was made.

The JDK debugger

The JDK debugger is called *jdb* and is used to search for errors in applications and applets. In the actual jdb version this is a simple program. If you are already familiar with the debugger of other programming languages, you will be disappointed. But it is still better than nothing.

To debug an application with the jdb, the javac compiler must add some special debugging information that the jbd debugger needs. Therefore, when compiling with javac, there is the option of -g, e.g.

```
Prompt> javac -g Error program.java
```

Now the program can be started in the debugger:

```
Prompt> jdb Error program
```

After loading and initialization, the jdb waits for the commands you input at the prompt (Table 16.4).

Command	Description
run	Starts the execution of the program.
stop at Class:Line	Puts a stop in the class class at line line .
stop in Class.Method	Puts a stop in the method of the class. It is stopped with the first statement of the method.
step	Executes a code line. Branches in method calls.
next	Executes a code line. Executes method calls as a command.
cont	Continues the execution of the program (after a stop).
list	Displays the source code.
locals	Display the local variables.
print Name	Displays the variable name.
where	Shows the sequence of the method calls.
quit	Exits jdb.
help	Gives a brief overview of all jdb commands.
!!	Repeats the last command.

Table 16.4: Important jdb commands.

> **CAUTION**
>
> *During the start of jdb, you could get a message that will try to establish a connection with the Internet. jdb requires an ongoing TCP/IP stack. If, in the Internet, you have a switched communication (dial-up connection) instead of a leased line, this is awkward and expensive because of telephone costs. Things are easier if you create a file called* hosts, *which contains the following line:*
>
> ```
> 127.0.0.1 localhost
> ```
>
> *This file has to be copied in the Windows 95/98 installations directory (usually* c:\windows*). In Linux, this file is usually already created in* /etc/hosts. *If it is not available, this line must be added.*

Outlook

If you have read the book and programmed the examples, you will have already learnt a lot about Java and the general bases of object-oriented programming: more than enough to develop and create your own program inspirations.

If you know that you are interested in the Java programming language, you will probably want to learn much more about Java and the possibilities of Java programming.

Java has a number of advanced concepts and programming techniques that we have left aside or just touched on quickly in this book. If you want to learn more about Java and find a book for advanced learners, make sure that the following themes are explained in detail:

- Inheritance of classes
- Overwriting of methods and polymorphism
- Implementation of interfaces
- Exceptions
- Threads
- Creation of GUI applications by means of AWT and Swing
- Programming of applets

We can recommend the following book:

- *Java 2 New Reference*, by Ralph Steyer

Appendix A

FAQs and typical errors

FAQs

What does FAQ mean?

FAQ stands for "frequently asked questions". The following are questions that almost all (Java) programmers ask at least once.

Why can I not compile my program? The source code is correct.

It is probably not correct (pay attention to details such as semicolons and brackets). A common error is forgetting the ending `.java` calling `javac myJavaFile.java`.

Why am I not able to start my compiled program?

The most common reason is the addition of the ending `.class` calling the interpreter. The correct version is `java myJavaFile`.

Java is already installed on my PC. How can I find out which version it is?

Open a console window and call `java - version` (without a file argument).

The javac compiler reports that I have not defined a constructor, even though there is one.

You have probably given a return value in the constructor. Constructors, however, have no return type, not even `void`.

The compiler outputs a warning that my program is using a *deprecated* method. What does this mean?

These are methods from the predefined Java package that have become obsolete and have been replaced with new methods. Deprecated methods are no longer supported in the long term and you should try to replace them with new methods. You get a list of the deprecated methods of a program if you call javac by means of the deprecation option.

What does the error message of javac "*can't make static reference to method ...*" mean?

This error occurs when a static method (e.g. `main()`) in the code tries to call another method that is not defined as `static`. Methods that are not `static` can only be called on an instance of the corresponding class.

Why are some classes defined with the access specificator `public` and others are not?

Explained simply, the access specificator `public` makes the declared class visible and usable to the outside world. Who is the outside world?

The outside world is, for instance, the Java interpreter that executes the program. Therefore, all main classes of our program are declared as `public` (for applications, the classes in which the `main()` method is defined, and for applets, the derived base class `Applet`).

If you create larger programs later, you will eventually begin to distribute the source text of the program among several source text files and organize it into packages. In doing so, you may define a class A in a package `PA` and use the source text in a package `PB`. Then you have to declare class A as `public`, because every other package belongs, according to the class, to the outside world.

What part do blank characters, tabulators and line breaks play in the source text?

They are used to separate identifiers and to define the source text clearly.

```
classHelloWorld
   {
```

Error: there should be a blank character between `class` and `HelloWorld`.

```
while(loop<2){++loop;System.out.println(loop);}
```

Correct, but ugly. Here you should insert blank characters and line breaks to improve readability.

Typical beginners' errors

Beginners often do not distinguish between capitalization and lower-case characters.

```
int myVar;
...
myvar = 1;
```

Here the compiler will find a fault, i.e. it will indicate that the identifier `myvar` was not introduced to it before.

Errors with the equals and assignment operators.

```
int i = 1;
...
if (i = 10)
  System.out.println("i : " + i);
...
```

The value of `i` is not compared with the value 10. Instead, the variable `i` is assigned to the value 10. An assignment, however, is no comparison and is not evaluated as a boolean value (`true` or `false`). Therefore, the compiler creates an error message.

Semicolons do not belong after the conditions of the if branching.

```
int i = 1;
...
if (i == 10);
   System.out.println("i : " + i);
...
```

The compiler interprets a semicolon placed after an `if` condition as a blank statement. In the example above, the `println` statement is always executed because from the point of view of the compiler, the `if` condition only controls the execution of the empty statement.

For the same reason, semicolons cannot be placed after the loop headers of the `for` and `while` loops.

```
int loop;
for (loop = 0; loop < 10; ++loop);
   {
   System.out.println(loop * loop);
   }
```

Here, the blank statement is executed ten times, but the `println` is only executed once.

The last element in an array with n elements has the index $n-1$. Access to the elements with a higher index (or with an index of less than 0) leads to runtime errors and generates an `ArrayIndexOutOfBounds` exception.

```
int[] field = new int[12];
int loop;
...
for (loop = 0; loop <= 12; ++loop);
   {
   field[loop] =  loop;
   }
```

Here, in the last loop passage, we try to write in the non-declared element `field[12]`.

The division of two integers returns an integer result even if the result of a `double` or `float` variable is assigned.

```
int value1 = 3;
int value2 = 4;
double result;

result = value1 / value2;   // results 0
```

To force a floating-point division at least one operand of the /operator has to be changed into a floating-point value:

```
int value1 = 3;
int value2 = 4;
double result;

result = (double) value1 / value2;  // results 0.75
```

Appendix B

Glossary

Access specifier
The access specificators `public`, `protected` and `private` are used to define classes and to control the class visibility and availability and its elements.

Applet
A Java program embedded in Web pages. If a browser requires this kind of Web page, the applet is obtained with the Web page by the Web server, loaded in the browser and executed by its integrated interpreter (provided that the browser has an integrated Java interpreter).

Arguments
Values that are submitted in the call of a method to the parameters of the method itself.

Array
Data structure in which you can join together several variables of one data type.

Block
One or more statements combined in curly brackets.

Branching
Program construction for the alternative execution of statement blocks.

Byte code
We define the "generic" (machine-independent) binary code created by the Java compiler as byte code.

Casting
Explicit type conversion.

Classes
Classes describe objects with general properties and methods. In Java, a class is a data type from which you can derive variables (instances).

Compiler
Program that converts the source text of a program into machine code (in Java, machine-independent byte code).

Concatenation
Appending strings to each other.

Console applications
Programs without any graphical interface that are usually called by the operating system console (in Windows, the MS-DOS prompt).

Constructor
Special methods that are called in the setting (instance creation) of the objects of the class.

Debugger
Program that can execute another program step by step.

Declaration
Execution and announcement of an identifier in a program source text.

Decrement
Degradation of the value of a variable by one unit.

Definition
Definition of an identifier (for a variable, method, type, etc.). For variables and methods, it is accompanied by the reservation of memory.

Derivation
We speak about derivation or inheritance when a new class is defined on the basis of an existing class (we call base or superior class). So, for example, the main class of an applet is usually derived from the Java class `Applet`.

Destructor
Special method `finalize()` that is called during the resolution of the objects of the class (counterpart of the constructor; it only has to be defined occasionally).

Encapsulation
Assuming that real objects are seen as existing features (data) and their methods in their representation in the program. The properties and methods of an object are combined in the class that the object represents.

Increment
Increase of the value of a variable by one unit.

Inheritance
Classes can be combined into class hierarchies. Derived classes adopt (inherit) the features and methods of the superordinated class.

Instance
Variable of a class type.

Instance variable
Variable that is declared in a class and contains a copy of each instance of that class.

Interfaces
Interfaces are collections of constant and method declarations, similar to classes. A class derived from an interface is obliged to implement all methods in the interface (i.e. to define statements sections).

Interpreter
Program that converts the code of a program into machine code and executes it.

Libraries
Collection of useful classes that you can use in a program.

Literal
Constants that are written as a value directly in the source text.

Loop
Program construct for the multiple execution of statement blocks.

Methods
Code blocks of a class provided with names. They implement the methods of the objects of the class.

Objects
The concept of object has different meanings in programming, depending on the context:

- In object-oriented models, we describe all real existing elements that later work with the program and for which we define classes as objects.

- In object-oriented programming, an object is the explicit manifestation of a class. You can access to an object on an instance (variable of type class).

- In the programming, we usually define data complexities that are stored in the memory as objects (storage objects)

Object orientation

In object-oriented programming, problems are solved by identifying objects, implementing them as classes and continuing to work with them. Most of the programming effort goes into the implementation of a suitable class for the representation of objects. The remainder of the program becomes simplified because later on, only the methods of the classes have to be called. In this process, methods are guaranteed to be executed correctly. The programmer should not be interested in the implementation of the class any more. Thanks to the classes, the resulting code is more easily understood, maintained and reused. Moreover, the object-oriented human way of seeing and classifying things is more suited to the elementary data types.

Overload

Overload is when several methods have the same name. Internally, the compiler consults the number and types of the parameters for the definite identification of the method that has to be called.

Overwriting

Renaming an inherited method in a derived class. The derived class then reacts to a corresponding method call in a specific way.

Package

Packages are used for the organization of the source text of larger programs. A class that is defined in a package can only be used in other packages when it has been declared as `public` (and contains a `public` element).

Parameters

Variables of a method that are declared in round brackets after the method name and are initialized when calling a method with the values that are submitted by the caller of the method (see Arguments).

Stream

Data stream between an input or output device and the program.

String

Character string.

Variable

An intermediate memory in which you can save values. Each variable has a name given through the declaration of the variable and on which you can query its actual value or assign a new value to it.

White space

The characters that create the blank spaces: blank characters, tabulators, line breaks.

Appendix C

Executing the sample program

You can find all the programs whose source texts are printed in the text with file names on the accompanying CD. There is a subdirectory for each chapter of the book. There, you will find the directories for the programs of each chapter. Finally, the source files are available in the program directory.

To execute one of the programs, proceed in the following way:

1 Copy the program directory from the accompanying cd onto your hard drive.

2 If necessary, assign the write protection for the files of the program.

In Windows, right-click on the Windows Explorer on the corresponding file and choose the FEATURES command in the context menu. When the option WRITE-PROTECTED appears in the dialogue field, deactivate the option.

In UNIX/Linux, you can set the access rights, for instance by using the system command `chmod`. Call a console, modify the source files and call `chmod` as follows: `chmod 777 filename.cpp`.

3 Open a console window, change to the corresponding directory (by means of the `cd` commands) and compile the program with javac. Finally, execute the program using the Java interpreter java (see also Chapter 3).

Appendix D

ASCII code and reserved keywords

ASCII code

Dec	Hex	Characters	Dec	Hex	Characters	Dec	Hex	Characters	Dec	Hex	Characters
0	00	NUL	32	20	SP	64	40	@	96	60	`
1	01	SOH	33	21	!	65	41	A	97	61	a
2	02	STX	34	22	"	66	42	B	98	62	b
3	03	ETX	35	23	#	67	43	C	99	63	c
4	04	EOT	36	24	$	68	44	D	100	64	d
5	05	ENQ	37	25	%	69	45	E	101	65	e
6	06	ACK	38	26	&	70	46	F	102	66	f
7	07	BEL	39	27	'	71	47	G	103	67	g
8	08	BS	40	28	(	72	48	H	104	68	h
9	09	HT	41	29	)	73	49	I	105	69	i
10	0A	NL	42	2A	*	74	4A	J	106	6A	j
11	0B	VT	43	2B	+	75	4B	K	107	6B	k
12	0C	NP	44	2C	,	76	4C	L	108	6C	l
13	0D	CR	45	2D	-	77	4D	M	109	6D	m
14	0E	SO	46	2E	.	78	4E	N	110	6E	n
15	0F	SI	47	2F	/	79	4F	O	111	6F	o
16	10	DLE	48	30	0	80	50	P	112	70	p
17	11	DC1	49	31	1	81	51	Q	113	71	q
18	12	DC2	50	32	2	82	52	R	114	72	r
19	13	DC3	51	33	3	83	53	S	115	73	s
20	14	DC4	52	34	4	84	54	T	116	74	t
21	15	NAK	53	35	5	85	55	U	117	75	u
22	16	SYN	54	36	6	86	56	V	118	76	v
23	17	ETB	55	37	7	87	57	W	119	77	w
24	18	CAN	56	38	8	88	58	X	120	78	x
25	19	EM	57	39	9	89	59	Y	121	79	y
26	1A	SUB	58	3A	:	90	5A	Z	122	7A	z
27	1B	ESC	59	3B	;	91	5B	[	123	7B	{
28	1C	FS	60	3C	<	92	5C	\	124	7C		
29	18	CAN	61	3D	=	93	5D	]	125	7D	}
30	19	EM	62	3E	>	94	5E	^	126	7E	~
31	1A	SUB	63	3F	?	95	5F	_	127	7F	DEL

Table D.1: The ASCII font.

Appendix E

Licence agreement

Sun Microsystems, Inc. Binary Code License Agreement

READ THE TERMS OF THIS AGREEMENT AND ANY PROVIDED SUPPLEMENTAL LICENSE TERMS (COLLECTIVELY "AGREEMENT") CAREFULLY BEFORE OPENING THE SOFTWARE MEDIA PACKAGE. BY OPENING THE SOFTWARE MEDIA PACKAGE, YOU AGREE TO THE TERMS OF THIS AGREEMENT. IF YOU ARE ACCESSING THE SOFTWARE ELECTRONICALLY, INDICATE YOUR ACCEPTANCE OF THESE TERMS BY SELECTING THE "ACCEPT" BUTTON AT THE END OF THIS AGREEMENT. IF YOU DO NOT AGREE TO ALL THESE TERMS, PROMPTLY RETURN THE UNUSED SOFTWARE TO YOUR PLACE OF PURCHASE OR, IF THE SOFTWARE IS ACCESSED ELECTRONICALLY, SELECT THE "DECLINE" BUTTON AT THE END OF THIS AGREEMENT.

1. LICENSE TO USE. Sun grants you a non-exclusive and non-transferable license for the internal use only of the accompanying software and documentation and any error corrections provided by Sun (collectively "Software"), by the number of users and the class of computer hardware for which the corresponding fee has been paid.

2. RESTRICTIONS Software is confidential and copyrighted. Title to Software and all associated intellectual property rights is retained by Sun and/or its licensors. Except as specifically authorized in any Supplemental License Terms, you may not make copies of Software, other than a single copy of Software for archival purposes. Unless enforcement is prohibited by applicable law, you may not modify, decompile, or reverse engineer Software. You acknowledge that Software is not designed, licensed or intended for use in the design, construction, operation or maintenance of any nuclear facility. Sun disclaims any express or implied warranty of fitness for such uses. No right, title or interest in or to any trademark, service mark, logo or trade name of Sun or its licensors is granted under this Agreement.

3. LIMITED WARRANTY. Sun warrants to you that for a period of ninety (90) days from the date of purchase, as evidenced by a copy of the receipt, the media on which Software is furnished (if any) will be free of defects in materials and workmanship under normal use. Except for the foregoing, Software is provided "AS IS". Your exclusive remedy and Sun's entire

liability under this limited warranty will be at Sun's option to replace Software media or refund the fee paid for Software.

4. DISCLAIMER OF WARRANTY. UNLESS SPECIFIED IN THIS AGREEMENT, ALL EXPRESS OR IMPLIED CONDITIONS, REPRESENTATIONS AND WARRANTIES, INCLUDING ANY IMPLIED WARRANTY OF MERCHANTABILITY, FITNESS FOR A PARTICULAR PURPOSE OR NON-INFRINGEMENT ARE DISCLAIMED, EXCEPT TO THE EXTENT THAT THESE DISCLAIMERS ARE HELD TO BE LEGALLY INVALID.

5. LIMITATION OF LIABILITY. TO THE EXTENT NOT PROHIBITED BY LAW, IN NO EVENT WILL SUN OR ITS LICENSORS BE LIABLE FOR ANY LOST REVENUE, PROFIT OR DATA, OR FOR SPECIAL, INDIRECT, CONSEQUENTIAL, INCIDENTAL OR PUNITIVE DAMAGES, HOWEVER CAUSED REGARDLESS OF THE THEORY OF LIABILITY, ARISING OUT OF OR RELATED TO THE USE OF OR INABILITY TO USE SOFTWARE, EVEN IF SUN HAS BEEN ADVISED OF THE POSSIBILITY OF SUCH DAMAGES. In no event will Sun's liability to you, whether in contract, tort (including negligence), or otherwise, exceed the amount paid by you for Software under this Agreement. The foregoing limitations will apply even if the above stated warranty fails of its essential purpose.

6. Termination. This Agreement is effective until terminated. You may terminate this Agreement at any time by destroying all copies of Software. This Agreement will terminate immediately without notice from Sun if you fail to comply with any provision of this Agreement. Upon Termination, you must destroy all copies of Software.

7. Export Regulations. All Software and technical data delivered under this Agreement are subject to US export control laws and may be subject to export or import regulations in other countries. You agree to comply strictly with all such laws and regulations and acknowledge that you have the responsibility to obtain such licenses to export, re-export, or import as may be required after delivery to you.

8. U.S. Government Restricted Rights. If Software is being acquired by or on behalf of the U.S. Government or by a U.S. Government prime contractor

or subcontractor (at any tier), then the Government's rights in Software and accompanying documentation will be only as set forth in this Agreement; this is in accordance with 48 CFR 227.7201 through 227.7202-4 (for Department of Defense (DOD) acquisitions) and with 48 CFR 2.101 and 12.212 (for non-DOD acquisitions).

9. Governing Law. Any action related to this Agreement will be governed by California law and controlling U.S. federal law. No choice of law rules of any jurisdiction will apply.

10. Severability. If any provision of this Agreement is held to be unenforceable, this Agreement will remain in effect with the provision omitted, unless omission would frustrate the intent of the parties, in which case this Agreement will immediately terminate.

11. Integration. This Agreement is the entire agreement between you and Sun relating to its subject matter. It supersedes all prior or contemporaneous oral or written communications, proposals, representations and warranties and prevails over any conflicting or additional terms of any quote, order, acknowledgment, or other communication between the parties relating to its subject matter during the term of this Agreement. No modification of this Agreement will be binding, unless in writing and signed by an authorized representative of each party.

For inquiries please contact:

Sun Microsystems, Inc.

901 San Antonio Road

Palo Alto, California 94303

U.S.A.

JAVA 2 SOFTWARE DEVELOPMENT KIT STANDARD EDITION VERSION 1.3 SUPPLEMENTAL LICENSE TERMS

These supplemental license terms ("Supplemental Terms") add to or modify the terms of the Binary Code License Agreement (collectively, the "Agreement"). Capitalized terms not defined in these Supplemental Terms shall have the same meanings ascribed to them in the Agreement. These Supplemental Terms shall supersede any inconsistent or conflicting terms in the Agreement, or in any license contained within the Software.

1. Internal Use and Development License Grant. Subject to the terms and conditions of this Agreement, including, but not limited to, Section 2 (Redistributables) and Section 4 (Java Technology Restrictions) of these Supplemental Terms, Sun grants you a non-exclusive, non-transferable, limited license to reproduce the Software for internal use only for the sole purpose of development of your JavaTM applet and application ("Program"), provided that you do not redistribute the Software in whole or in part, either separately or included with any Program.

2. Redistributables. In addition to the license granted in Paragraph 1 above, Sun grants you a non-exclusive, non-transferable, limited license to reproduce and distribute, only as part of your separate copy of JAVA(TM) 2 RUNTIME ENVIRONMENT STANDARD EDITION VERSION 1.3 software, those files specifically identified as redistributable in the JAVA(TM) 2 RUNTIME ENVIRONMENT STANDARD EDITION VERSION 1.3 "README" file (the "Redistributables") provided that: (a) you distribute the Redistributables complete and unmodified (unless otherwise specified in the applicable README file), and only bundled as part of the JavaTM applets and applications that you develop (the "Programs:); (b) you do not distribute additional software intended to supersede any component(s) of the Redistributables; (c) you do not remove or alter any proprietary legends or notices contained in or on the Redistributables; (d) you only distribute the Redistributables pursuant to a license agreement that protects Sun's interests consistent with the terms contained in the Agreement; and (e) you agree to defend and indemnify Sun and its licensors from and against any damages, costs, liabilities, settlement amounts and/or expenses (including attorneys' fees) incurred in connection with any claim, lawsuit or action by any third party that arises or results from the use or distribution of any and all Programs and/or Software.

3. Separate Distribution License Required. You understand and agree that you must first obtain a separate license from Sun prior to reproducing or modifying any portion of the Software other than as provided with respect to Redistributables in Paragraph 2 above.

4. Java Technology Restrictions. You may not modify the Java Platform Interface ("JPI", identified as classes contained within the "java" package or any subpackages of the "java" package), by creating additional classes within the JPI or otherwise causing the addition to or modification of the classes in the JPI. In the event that you create an additional class and associated API(s) which (i) extends the functionality of a Java environment, and (ii) is exposed to third party software developers for the purpose of developing additional software which invokes such additional API, you must promptly publish broadly an accurate specification for such API for free use by all developers. You may not create, or authorize your licensees to create additional classes, interfaces, or subpackages that are in any way identified as "java", "javax", "sun" or similar convention as specified by Sun in any class file naming convention. Refer to the appropriate version of the Java Runtime Environment binary code license (currently located at http://www.java.sun.com/jdk/index.html) for the availability of runtime code which may be distributed with Java applets and applications.

5. Trademarks and Logos. You acknowledge and agree as between you and Sun that Sun owns the Java trademark and all Java-related trademarks, service marks, logos and other brand designations including the Coffee Cup logo and Duke logo ("Java Marks"), and you agree to comply with the Sun Trademark and Logo Usage Requirements currently located at http://www.sun.com/policies/trademarks. Any use you make of the Java Marks inures to Sun's benefit.

6. Source Code. Software may contain source code that is provided solely for reference purposes pursuant to the terms of this Agreement.

7. Termination. Sun may terminate this Agreement immediately should any Software become, or in Sun's opinion be likely to become, the subject of a claim of infringement of a patent, trade secret, copyright or other intellectual property right.

Index